HUMANITY

The Philosophy For The 21ˢᵗ Century

HUMAN ETHICS, HUMAN DUTIES
and
HUMAN RIGHTS

Author
D.V. Natekar

©
Shri. D. V. Natekar
Flat No. 4, Bldg. No. 19,
Anandnagar, Paud Road,
Pune 411029.
Phone : 91-020-25442404
Mobile : 09225631101
E-mail : natekardilip@yahoo.com

Second Edition : 2021
ISBN : 978-93-5265-458-1 (Paper Back)
ISBN : 978-93-5265-459-8 (Electronic)

Type Setting :
Modern Printing Press
1358A, Shukrawar Peth,
Pune 411002.

Printing :
Modern Printing Service
1358A, Shukrawar Peth,
Pune 411002.
E-mail : balodyanpress@gmail.com

PRICE : Rs. 200/- (Paper Back)
       Rs. 100/- (Electronic)

CONTENTS

FOREWORD

There are radical changes in ideas, thoughts, ambitions, customs, needs and expectations of human beings in last 100 years. Development and progress of human and humanity is the motto of today's era.

Liberal views, tolerance, openness and transparency are helpful for development of mankind. It is essential to develop liking for truthfulness, morality and beauty.

This book is written with the hope that it may help, to develop individuals with high morality, scientific, logical, truthful and altruistic attitude and liberal, tolerant and peaceful society.

The entire mankind on this earth should be united as one family. The need of the hour is to develop mutual goodwill, trust and understanding for peaceful coexistence. Race, religion, nationality, creed, colour, languages, states, castes have divided the mankind into various factions for thousands of years. All these factions can come together under the umbrella of HUMANITY.

The first chapter briefs on human society and explains working of the mind with a unique working diagram. Mankind has to adjust with the adverse circumstances, keep a ray of hope in a distressed, depressed situation, have courage to face calamities, create enthusiasm and look for joy and happiness in every aspect of life. This is possible only if he develops a strong, firm, balanced and calm mind. The understanding of working of mind, it's enemies and disorders helps him to get a strong mind.

The second chapter gives us the cream, the principles of humanity. The principles of humanity comprises of globally acceptable ethics, duties and rights of human beings.

Mankind has wasted a huge amount of energy, money and time on imaginary concepts of three storey set up of heaven at the top, earth in the middle and hell at the bottom. The third chapter, briefs on the imaginary concepts of heaven, hell, soul, rebirth, ghosts, satan, god and miracles. One religion is no solution to another religion. Religion and ritual free world is the real solution. Hence the earlier name of the book "Humanity-The religion for the 21ˢᵗ Century" is renamed by replacing the word "religion" by the word "philosophy" while revising for the third edition..

The process of how things happen, is explained in chapter IV.

Entire life is spent in pursuit of happiness. Is anybody happy? Is gratification happiness? The 'fun loving', 'enjoyment loving', hedonist folks finally claim that they have not got the much sought after happiness and contentment. Chapter five tries to elaborate on happiness.

After the philosophical part of the 5 chapters the various values of life , along with the important aspects like sports, art, knowledge, the most serious threat to mankind in 21ˢᵗ century of population explosion and vices like theft, corruption, addiction, gambling are elaborated in the descriptive part.

My sincere gratitude to my parents and guardian sisters for contributing toward development of moral, benevolent, scientific, global and logical attitude.

Let us make this planet a better place to live!

17ᵗʰ January 2017   **D. V. Natekar**

Population figures are updated and text corrected/revised wherever found necessary.

All parables at the end of the chapter are from internet or social media.

17th September 2021   **D V Natekar**

1 HUMAN SOCIETY AND HUMAN MIND

1.1 HISTORY OF HUMAN SOCIETY-

Before considering today's human society, we shall consider a brief history of the mankind on this planet for the last 10,000 years.

The human beings are on this planet for over 150,000 years He invented how to make fire thousands of years back. Primitive boats also appear to have been invented long time back.

Flocks of human beings- Man lived in caves. Like flocks of animals, earlier human beings lived in flocks. There were no relations like father, mother, brother, sister etc. Various sounds that a human being could produce were the language. Agriculture had not taken birth. 'Wheel' was unknown. No metal was known. This period dates back to approximately 10,000 years before Christ.

Matriarchal System- Children born of a woman started living together. This was a period of polyandry, with a woman heading the group predominantly formed by her daughters and sons. Thus mother, brother and sister were the relations existing. Agriculture and domestication of some animals began. Human started settling around rivers as a source of water for agriculture and drinking. Thus began the human civilization. Script based on pictures started. Man came out from caves and started building his shelter using animal skins, parts of trees and then stones. Animal skin, leaves and bark skins were used as clothes. This era was approximates 8,000 to 10,000 B.C.

Patriarchal System- Like monkeys, the most powerful man of the group or flock started controlling the group. Languages started originating. Script of straight and curved lines started. Agriculture was established. Gold, Silver and Copper became known to the mankind. This was a period of predominant polygamy. Use of animals for transport, wool and milk started. This was a period of approx. 5,000 to 8,000 B.C.

Family System- Kings and Kingdoms came into existence.

Demerits of polyandry and polygamy were understood and one wife-one husband family system started. The institution of marriage was established. The foundations of the various sciences like agriculture, medicine, astronomy, metallurgy, textile etc. were laid. Concepts of God, ghosts, heaven, hell, soul, Satan, and life after death were formulated. This was a period approx. from 3,000 to 5,000 B.C

Period of Cultural development- Morality, ethics, good behaviour, good thoughts and so many concepts in philosophy were developed by great philosophers like Plato, Aristotle, Srikrishna, Gautam Buddha, Zoroaster, Mahavir, Jesus Christ, Mohammed Paigambar etc. The foundation of basic needs of food, clothing, shelter, medicine and education were laid. The state administration mainly through King and Kingdom system was established. There was tremendous development in Astronomy, languages, scripts, arts and craft, medicine, textile etc. This was a period from 3,000 BC to 1,600 AD approx..

Beginning of industrialization- Mankind particularly in Europe laid the foundation of industrialization and basic sciences of physics, chemistry and biology. There were tremendous improvements in harnessing animal power, construction of buildings, agriculture, textile, shipping and universal trade. Europeans spread all over the world from North and South America to Africa, Asia and Australia. This was the beginning of globalization of science and technology, of clothing and trade, of language and culture. This planet became known to mankind in the real sense and maps were prepared. This was a period from 1,600 AD to 1900 AD approx.

20ᵗʰ Century- Exponential development in science and technology took place in the 20ᵗʰ century. Manifold knowledge was acquired by mankind in these 100 years than previous 10,000 years. Over 100 elements and millions of their compounds were available to mankind. Aeroplanes, helicopters, buses, cars, scooters, motorcycles, ships, bicycles were invented for faster and easier transport. Due to tremendous development in physics, chemistry, biology the laws of nature were learnt by mankind. Electricity, Magnetic energy, Atomic Energy, Heat, light and mechanical energy were available to the mankind as never before. Communication improved exponentially with telephones, telexes, telefaxes, and radio and satellite communications. There was tremendous development in construction of roads, houses and bridges. Medicine and medical science improved tremendously with eradication of many diseases and improvement of life expectancy of human beings with overall better health. Standard of living tremendously improved with radios, TVs, VCRs, CD players, washing machines, vacuum cleaners, refrigerators, fluorescent lamps, cooking gas, irons, water heaters making daily life of human beings more comfortable, more assured and more peaceful. Technology of mass production, use of computers in manufacturing, design, finance and material control, improvement in agricultural yield, technologies for generation and utilisation of electrical energy led to development of mankind which could not be even dreamt of a century ago. Journey to the moon was a great footstep ahead for the mankind.

These advantages were offset by population explosion creating ever increasing wants and an increasing scarcity of food and shelter. More powerful arms and higher difference in standard of living increased crime, gambling, adultery, terrorism, oppression and exploitation. Environmental deterioration, air and noise pollution, contamination of water, adulteration of food and drugs, destructive atomic weapons, RDX type explosives leading to killing and destruction has made this planet a worse place to live.

1.2 TODAY'S HUMAN SOCIETY-

Man is a social animal. In early period, human beings used to depend on each other for self protection as well as for the protection of their children, for gathering of food and shelter with each others help.

As human beings progressed, interdependence increased. Today's human being is dependent on each other for food, building of shelter, clothing, education, health, protection, law and order, commerce, electricity, petrol, minerals, plastics, chemicals, electronic instruments, transport, communication, sports, milk, newspaper etc.

Recollect your daily routine. You cannot spend a day unless you indirectly take benefit of services of a few hundred people. Are you aware that when you buy a small handkerchief at least a few hundred human beings must have worked to produce it? The cotton farmer, people working on his farm for ploughing, seeding, watering, spraying insecticides, giving manure and fertilizers, seed producers and marketers, insecticide and fertilizer producers and hundreds of workers working for them, tractor manufacturers, producers of iron, rubber, aluminum parts used, workers in the mines, electricity producers, irrigation canal workers, various banks and financial institutions financing the various people above, various Govt. Departments like irrigation, power, agriculture, fertilizer, commerce and finance. Thus, behind just a handkerchief there are hundreds of human beings involved.

With today's means of transport and communication human society on this planet which grew from flocks, villages, townships, kingdoms to nations has slowly turned into one family. Natural calamities like cyclones, earthquakes or serious accidents of trains, aeroplanes or ships bring the whole world- the entire human community on this earth- together to help the needy without any consideration of nation, race, religion, caste, creed or gender. Similar coming together is also seen in case of natural phenomena like the solar eclipse or international sport events such as Olympics or world cup football.

Unfortunately today's human society is in serious trouble as it is engulfed by crime, corruption, adultery, terrorism, exploitation, oppression, gambling and addiction. Under the cover of "fun and enjoyment" destructive tendencies are getting strengthened. Every effort should be made at individual, family, social, political, judicial and administrative level to curb these tendencies both nationally and internationally.

The biggest problem of today's society is population explosion. The human population grew from 500 million in the 16th century to 1650 million at the beginning of the 20th century and we entered the 21st century with the human population around 6000 million! How much human population can this planet sustain? For how many people can this earth provide food, water and place to live? Considering the needs of human being this earth can sustain at the most 4500 million human beings. Any population, more than that, would lead to ecological imbalance and destruction.

To achieve this, the birth rate should be restricted to 6.25 per thousand per year. This can only be achieved if we strictly follow the principle of "one man one wife, one woman one husband and one couple one child". Once the population comes down below 4500 million, the birth rates and death rates can be reviewed. If we consider uniform distribution of age in the society, average life expectancy of 80 years will give death rate of 12.5 and with life expectancy of 70 years the death rate will be 14 to 15 per 1000. For reduction in population birth rate has to be lower than death rate.

The main problems before today's society are to maintain ecological balance, to prevent pollution of air, water and sound, to ensure proper supply of water, proper sanitation and to prevent adulteration of food.

If average life expectancy is considered to be 80 years, the initial 20 years are spent in childhood and education and last 20 years are spent in old age. Out of the balance 40 years the human being can work with full vigour and fitness for 20 years and with partial fitness from age 40 to 60. In short, almost 50% of their life human beings are dependent for their physical, psychological and financial needs on others. This divides human life into 4 different age groups.

UP TO 20 YEARS OF AGE-

During this period of physical and mental growth parents / guardians / family / society have to provide food, shelter, clothes, education, knowledge, skill as nicely as possible. Putting this age group for work for earnings should be avoided.

AGE GROUP 20 TO 40-

Hard work for creative and constructive contribution to society for development, progress of mankind and supporting other groups as well as themselves is the main function of this age group.

AGE GROUP 40 TO 60-

To work, though may be with lesser power but with more experience guiding the juniors and giving some time for society.

AGE 60 AND ABOVE-

Guide, encourage and provide psychological support to society.

If we do not accept the above reality we not only suffer physically but psychologically as well.

1.3 THE INSTITUTION OF FAMILY-

A closely knit group of human beings having direct or indirect blood relation forms a family. Family is the foundation of society. Family originates from marriage. Marriage represents integrity, honesty and everlastingness of relationship and not just union of two human beings. It is an institution that connects and bonds human beings. The importance and effect of this institution are far reaching and are of immense value to society and obviously far outweighs just unison of two human beings. Stronger the family, stronger is the society. Family institution imparts the primary education of self sacrifice and compromise and leads towards individual development and progress with mutually complimentary and supplementary functions.

If you assume an average life of 80 years of a human being at least during the first 18 years it needs the support of parents or guardians not only for food, clothing, shelter, educational and health needs but also for psychological and moral needs.

Patience, cooperation, understanding, consideration and sacrifice lead to strong family relations.

Each and every member of family should compliment and supplement the functions and responsibilities of the other members. The piety of the institution of marriage should not be destroyed by involving transaction of money, properties, ornaments and other commercial interests. Blood group, thoughts, customs, financial, educational, health and emotional background must be considered before establishing a marital relationship.

Once the relationship is established it should be mutually treated with piety and respect and divorce should be avoided except in very very exceptional cases of impotence, serious illness, physical or mental disability, adultery and mental and physical harassment beyond normal tolerance. Divorce should be avoided after having children and if marriage is 10-15 years old the other factors should also be overlooked.

1.4 HUMAN RELATIONS-

We have seen interdependence of human beings. We take the benefit of the service of hundreds of people everyday. We have also seen that over a few hundred people are indirectly involved in providing us with a small handkerchief.

Thus, every human being interacts daily directly or indirectly with many other human beings. It is not a physical but a mental interaction.

Interaction of two or more minds of human beings is known as human relations.

Hence if we want to study human beings, human society, humanity, then we must understand human mind, its working, its disorders. The study of human mind is important also from the point of view that it is the "human mind" that needs to be conditioned to achieve safe and peaceful life. Let us try to understand the human mind.

1.5 WORKING OF HUMAN MIND-

Brain and nervous system is like the "hardware" of a computer and human mind is the "software" in it. In still simpler language, the brain and nervous system is like a wire/cable conducting electricity and mind is like the electricity flowing through that wire.

The mind- of human beings and other animals- basically consists of two main parts-

1) Logic,

2) Memory

Memory is basically of two types- short term memory and long term memory. Each and every happening of a day goes into memory but most things are forgotten by the end of the day. If you try to recollect the happenings of a day, only a few are recollected. You can remember what you had for breakfast today, may be yesterday or two days back but we cannot remember what we ate a week or a fortnight back in general, whereas a specific meal that you had 40 years back can be clearly remembered. It is very difficult to say what one would remember for a short time and what would be remembered for a long time. But in general very peculiar matters or incidents involving very high emotions of sadness or anger or happiness may be remembered for ever.

Logic can also be divided into only two main categories viz.-

1. Ego
2. Desire to live

When "ego" supersedes "Desire to live" a human being sacrifices his life for his country or for his "Kith and Kin" or himself (suicide). When "Desire to live" supersedes "ego" the human being accepts slavery or oppression or exploitation.

The outside (the body) world is known to human being through the five senses.

1. Sight
2. Smell
3. Hearing
4. Taste
5. Touch

All these sensations are stored in memory.

The output of human mind is exhibited in five ways(Attitudes)

1. Behaviour
2. Thought
3. Emotion
4. Perception
5. Personality

Personality does not mean only the appearance, colour, shape, looks, style of talking and walking but also includes the way a person behaves, thinks, his emotional responses, his memory and intelligence. Intelligence is the continuous interaction of the five senses, five attitudes, memory and logic. It involves analysis, synthesis, sequencing, classification, discretion, correlation, interlinking, reasoning, decision making etc.

INSTINCT is the genetically transmitted programme built in mind. LIFE'S MAIN AIM IS CONDITIONING OF MIND FOR DEVELOPMENT OF VIRTUES AND ELIMINATION OF VICES.

Now let us prepare a block diagram from the above information to enable us to understand the "MIND".

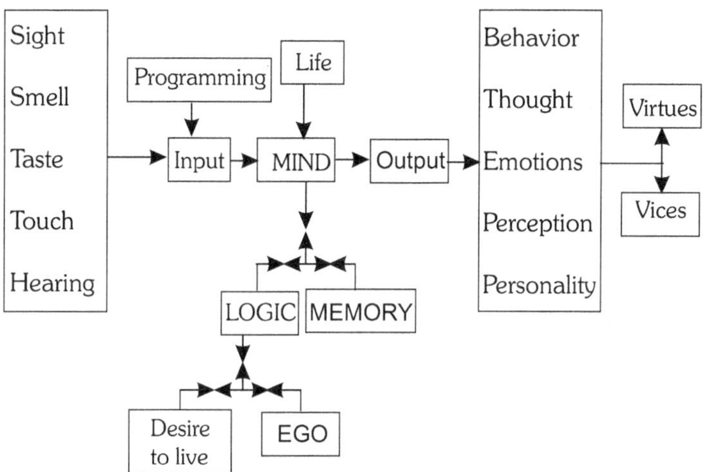

Now let us have a look at the block diagram of a computer given below.

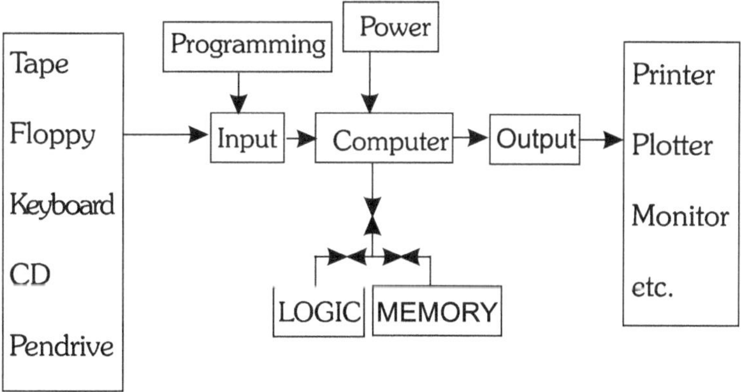

One can notice from the above that the basic block diagram of the mind and a computer is the same. Mind is a 'Super Computer'. We can know and understand more about the mind by studying and understanding the computer. Computer is purely electronic whereas mind works on electro-chemical reactions in the brain.

Intelligence develops output of the mind based on the input from the 5 senses, memory and basic logic. Just as the output of a computer depends on the synthesis and analysis of the input, based on its programming, similarly the output from the human mind in terms of behaviour, thought, emotion, perception and personality depends on "programming" of the human mind. This programming of the mind, which is nothing, but to inculcate and imbibe the values of life on the human mind, that should result in the development of virtues and elimination of vices. If wrong values of life are inculcated, it would result in development of vices rather than virtues!

The internal working of the mind is perceived through the gait, gestures, the speech, changes in eyes, face and voice.

1.6 VIRTUES and VICES-

One line phylosophy of life is "Try to be a good human being." How? By eliminating the vices and developing the virtues.

(a) Purpose of development of virtues and elimination of vices is to make human life safe, peaceful, happy, contented, and beneficial to entire mankind.

(b) Whether a particular attribute is a virtue or a vice is determined by the "cause and effect" analysis or in other words motive or purpose behind it and its ultimate effect on an individual, society and the whole mankind. Section 2.7 explaining 'ego' as a virtue and ego as a vice, may help one to understand the same. Balanced and firm intelligence is needed to fully understand the same.

(c) Virtue means void of desire and aversion. Virtue is conduct free from malice, anger and bitter speech. Virtues sum the things that should be done and vices sum the things that should be shunned. The chief virtue is not to do any evil knowingly, to any person at any time, even to the lowest degree.

Vices	**Virtues**
1. Falsehood	Truthfulness
2. Violence	Non Violence
3. Wickedness	Love
4. Cruelty	Compassion/kindness
5. Vengefulness	Forgiveness
6. Lack of peace	Peace
7. Belligerence	Peace
8. Slavery	Liberty
9. Inequality	Equality
10. Enmity	Fraternity
11. Injustice	Justice
12. Immorality	Morality
13. Ego	Control of ego
14. Selfishness	Altruism
15. Malevolent	Benevolent
16. Ungratefulness	Gratitude
17. Narrow minded	Liberal
18. Misery	Generosity
19. Deceit	Sincerity
20. Disloyalty	Loyalty
21. Treason	Integrity
22. Treachery	Fidelity
23. Disharmony	Harmony
24. Dishonesty	Honesty
25. Crookedness	Straight forwardness
26. Nonchalance	Enthusiasm
27. Hypocrisy	Reality
28. Vanity	Simplicity
29. Adulteration	Purity
30. Eccentricity	Equanimity
31. Impatience/Haste	Patience
32. Ferociousness	Calmness
33. Unpleasantness	Pleasantness
34. Fickleness	Firmness
35. Hesitance / suspicion	stead fastness

36.	Indecency	Gentleness / decency
37.	Lack of duty sense	Dutifulness
38.	Discontentment	Contentment
39.	Dissatisfaction	Satisfaction
40.	Vagabond	Penance
41.	Hedonism	Sacrifice
42.	Intolerance	Tolerance
43.	Ill feeling / Malevolence	Goodwill
44.	Inconsistency	Consistency
45.	Shallowness	Dedication
46.	Lack of devotion	Devotion
47.	Lack of determination	Determination
48.	Indiscipline	Discipline
49.	Shirking from work	Diligence
50.	Ridicule	Praise
51.	Desire	Control of desire
52.	Passion / lust	freedom from lust
53.	Anger	Calmness
54.	Greed	Control of senses
55.	Temptation	Control of mind
56.	Arrogance / Adamance	Modesty / humility
57.	Jealousy	Appreciation
58.	Envy	Admiration
59.	Abhorrence	Love
60.	Hatred	Affection
61.	Fear	Fearlessness
62.	Theft	Freedom from theft
63.	Addiction	Freedom from addiction
64.	Gambling	Freedom from gambling
65.	Corruption	Non corruption
66.	Adultery / debauchery	Austerity
67.	Disrespect	Respect
68.	Selfishness	Selflessness
69.	Terrorism	Peaceful coexistence
70.	Cowardice	Courage
71.	Timidness	Bravery

72.	Pessimist	Optimist
73.	Non cooperation	Cooperation
74.	Shabbiness	Cleanliness
75.	Non-sportmanship	Sportsmanship
76.	Lack of faith	Faith
77.	Laziness	Alertness
78.	Humiliation	Compassion

Everyday, if one goes through the above list and thinks before sleeping about the vices to which he or she was exposed to, during the day and thinks after getting up about the virtues that he / she would stick to during the day, there would be miraculous improvement in the attitudes of the concerned person. This way improvement in an individual would lead to improvement of a group and improvement in several groups would lead to the improvement of society and improvements in societies would lead to improvement of mankind.

Whether a particular attitude can be a vice or a virtue can be decided by the motive or purpose behind it and its overall effect on individual, society or mankind.

In order to understand this let us consider 'EGO' the basic logic in the minds of all living things.

1.7 EGO-

Ego is the basic logic of the mind. It is an inseparable part of all living things. Even cats and dogs display ego.

A human being strives to improve his behaviour due to ego. Ego makes people excel in various fields such as educational, social, cultural, sports. One wishes to overcome vices and develop virtues because of ego.

If the same ego is not controlled by balance of mind and conscience, it results in a stream of vices like arrogance, adamance, lust, anger, killing, violence, enmity, crookedness, vengefulness and so on.

One should not forget that the way your ego prompts you to concentrate on 'I', 'me' and 'mine' every other living thing has his 'ego' prompting the same. Whenever two or more living things meet, their egos clash and a satisfactory compromise of 'egos' takes place. Ego has a hard time meeting and satisfying the conflicting demands of the world outside i.e. external reality. To succeed even partially the ego must make certain compromises in its own defense. These compromises are called as mental mechanisms or mental dynamisms.

If a balanced mind and conscience do not control ego, then gratification of desires becomes the highest goal. These demonic desires make one forget about the rightful and just means in pursuit of wealth and power. "I" will get this. Then that will also be "mine". Everybody will work for "me". I will enjoy whatever materialistic pleasures those are available on this earth. All desires of all my senses shall be satisfied! I will be the richest, strongest person holding all reigns of power! 'I', 'me' and 'mine'... that's all!

Finally desires grow exponentially and reach such a devastating stage that you neither have physical nor mental strength and time to satisfy all desires. Whatever has been done in pursuit of happiness, enjoyment and fun ultimately leads to dissatisfaction, unhappiness, sadness, disillusion, anger and abhorrence.

When a balanced, firm and controlled mind develops ego as a virtue which leads one to excel in any field such as science, education, sports and destroys "ego as a vice" which leads to pride, prejudice and desires or cravings, one ultimately leads a happy, contented and peaceful life.

Whether 'ego' is a 'virtue' or a 'vice' is decided by the purpose or motive behind it and its ultimate effect on the individual, society and entire mankind.

In order to further understand the 'mind' of a human being, let us try to understand in brief the disorders of the mind.

1.8 DISORDERS OF MIND-

Disorders of the mind are basically disorders of attitudes.

1.8.1 *Disorders of behaviour-*

(i) Over activity- shouting, throwing, beating someone etc.

(ii) Retarded activity- avoiding work, doing things exactly opposite to what you are told, refusing work.

(iii) Morbid impulses- Kleptomania - Desire to steel

Dipsomania - Uncontrolled craving for liquor.

Pyromania - Desire to set fire.

1.8.2 *Disorders of emotions-*

(i) Euphoria - Feeling of excess joy, contentment.

(ii) Melancholia - state of mind in which fear, anxiety, worry, indecision, pessimism, brooding, unwillingness to act, feeling of wretchedness, depression, dejection, dominates individual mental outlook.

(iii) Apathy - No response to surroundings which should cause joy or sorrow to an average person. It is a typical case of a widow described in a poem, when the dead body of her husband was brought home, as "She must weep or she may die."

1.8.3 *Disorders of thought-*

(i) Delusion- that the person is superhuman.
That the person is not loved.
That the person is being tortured.
That the person is being deformed.
That the person is being harmed.
That the person is being poisoned etc.

(ii) Obsession - Some idea continuously fills the persons mind which are very difficult to get rid of in spite of the fact that outwardly the person is fully convinced about the futility or falsehood of idea.

Delusion and obsession lead to suspicion and prejudice, and these two are more harmful for peaceful, safe and happy living than anything else.

1.8.4. *Disorders of perception-*

(i) Hallucination - Seeing ghosts, gods, dead persons, animals, imaginary persons etc. where nothing exists.

(ii) Illusion - Seeing ghosts, gods, dead persons, animals, imaginary persons etc. where something exists.
Thus, when you see a snake which is not there or see a ghost when nothing exists, it is hallucination, but when you see a snake in the place of rope or you see a ghost in place of a tree or a man it is an illusion.

(iii) Paranoia - person firmly believes that he is some great person like Napoleon or George Washington.

(iv) Agar phobia - Fear of open space.

(v) Claustrophobia - Fear of closed space etc.

1.8.5 *Disorders of memory-*

(i) Amnesia - Loss of memory

(ii) Hyperaesthesia - Morbid / excessive sensitiveness.

1.8.6 *Disorders of personality -*

(i) Depersonalisation - The person forgets his own identity.

(ii) Transformation - The person feels he is someone else, it is necessarily paranoia - if he feels he is some great person.

(iii) Split personality - (Schizophrenia) two different personalities - one kind, loving and sympathetic and the other rude, arrogant and non sympathetic residing in a single person's mind. A typical case of "Kick the subordinates and lick the boss!"

The above information on disorders of mind is given only with a view to enable one to understand the mind better.

1.9 CONTROL OF THE MIND-

We have now seen how the mind functions. The mind expresses itself in terms of behaviour, thought, emotion, perception and personality. Good programming results in the cultural development that develops virtues and eliminates vices. Improper programming of the mind results in a perverted mind and cultivation of vices and lessening of virtues.

Control of mind results from inculcating values of life, imbibing importance of virtues and their development and guarding against vices. Control of mind is effected through external programming as well as through internal programming.

External programming comes through education in schools, guidance from parents, learning from the society where you live, from reading, listening, observing etc.

Internal programming is self-thought - when there is no input from the senses and no output from the body. There is continuous interaction between the memory and basic logics - ego and desire to live. Your intelligence is at work! Understanding, analysing, sequencing, grading, comparing, forming opinion, discretion, conscience, imagination, will power, planning etc. all form the part of this phenomenon.

You can never control your mind, unless the external programming is supplemented by internal programming.

What is control of the mind? To control the desire of senses - lust, anger, greed, adamance, jealousy, temptation and ego means to control the mind. You need a great discipline, determination, devotion, dedication and sacrifice to achieve control of the mind.

How can one recognise if he has achieved control of mind?

 (i) Restrained and balanced mind can think of both sides of the coin and understand the motive and effects of any action. Thus equanimity is achieved.

 (ii) Intelligence is stabilized. You never have doubts (e.g. 'to be or not to be') You get firmness, steadfastness. You can take firm decision without wavering.

(iii) Intelligence can act judiciously, can discriminate between good and bad, just and unjust, truth and falsehood. Thought can control emotions.

(iv) You get freedom from greed, temptation and lust.

 (v) You get freedom from ego and associated possessiveness.

(vi) If you restraint your ego, desires and aversions you have achieved control of the mind. The ultimate status referred to as "liberated" or "self realized" mind is the stage when possessiveness desires and aversions are not generated at all in the mind!

Self-awareness and meditation help in control of mind.

1.10 CONTROL OF DESIRES AND 'ENEMIES' OF THE MIND-

There are six 'enemies' of the mind.

 (i) Lust or excessive sexual desire,

 (ii) Temptation or mental desire,

(iii) Greed or desire of the senses,

(iv) Anger arising out of the above three desires,

 (v) Adamance or arrogance arising out of ego,

(vi) Jealousy arising out of ego and desires.

1.10.1 *Lust or passion* - Every adult, particularly during youth, naturally gets sexual instinct. Every living organism is capable of giving birth to another living being of its species - whether it is a microscopic amoeba giving birth by division, or birds coming out from eggs or mammals giving birth to babies. Sexual instinct is a combination of the basic logic of 'ego' and 'desire to live' and is natural and inherent.

Early human beings were having free sex like other animals. As human beings became more and more civilised and culture evolved they realized they are mentally and physically different from other animals. During childhood and old age humans depend on society in general and on previous and successive generation in particular. Other animals can recognise relations like 'my father', 'my brother', 'my mother', 'my sister' etc. for a small period of time whereas a human being can recognise this for its life time. The possessive attitude of 'my son', 'my wife' involves emotions and sentiments that are mostly absent in other animals. All these factors viz.

(a) Possessiveness,
(b) Emotions,
(c) Dependence for the first quarter of life on the previous generation,
(d) Dependence for the last quarter of life on the successive generation,
(e) Use of clothes by civilised humans not only for protection from weather but also to meet the norms of decency and modesty of civilised society.
(f) Confusion, enmity, fights, killings arising from free sex.

led to the formation of the institution of marriage and the system of "family".

In animals limited periods of heat and continuous fear of death restricted and limited population growth as well as controlled sexual excesses. In civilised human beings this is controlled through-

(i) Institution of marriage,
(ii) Family system,
(iii) Necessity of solitude,
(iv) Code of conduct for morality,
(v) Laws and legislation of the country,
(vi) Fear of contracting sexually transmitted diseases like

gonorrhoea, syphilis, AIDs etc,

(vii) Fear of disturbing EGO,

(viii) Fear of death, etc..

Every civilised human being should keep his lust/passion under control. No one should have sex below 18 years of age. Sexual relation with any person with whom you are not married, should not only be deplored morally but legally as well and should have severe punishment. If right from childhood the mind is inculcated against adultery then your character buildup would always control your lust.

It must be borne in mind that the 21st century morality standard for the family based on "monogamy" and "monoandry" (one man-one wife and conversely one woman-one husband) has been developed over the last 5,000 years. This not only helps healthy growth of children but reduces crime, violence, gambling, addiction and terrorism in society. One who has enjoyed safety, security, bond of love and sharing, pride and reputation of his family would seldom approach a path leading to vices.

Finally this discipline is going to help mankind to maintain a population of 4,500 million on this planet. If population goes beyond 4,500 million it takes us to scarcity, want and unhappiness.

1.10.2 *Temptation or mental desire-*

Temptation arises from ego. The basic needs of water, food, clean air, shelter, clothing, health and education multiply exponentially due to ego.

You want better and clean air? Come on let's go to this "beach", then to that "hill station" and then to a "holiday resort" on an Island. You keep on searching for better and better and the search never ends! You never get satisfied. The more you chase comforts and pleasures the more away you are from contentment.

Ordinary water is no good! You need different cold drinks.

'My' drink should be better than that of others. 'My food should be the best. 'My' shelter should be a classic piece of architecture! 'I' should have a better furnished house than others. Even if 'I' cough 'I' will go to the topmost physician. Even for cold 'I' will get admitted to a hospital with "5 star" facilities.

Maximum temptation is for power, money and wealth. In pursuit of money some people tend to follow any path including corruption, theft, extortion. Gambling is the bane of mankind in pursuit of money. People gamble through lottery, horse racing, and in shares to get rich fast.

Are you going to get satisfaction and happiness when you get the money? Not at all!! Temptation continuous and grows from thousands to millions to billions and so on. From walking to a bicycle, from a bicycle to a moped, from a moped to a motorcycle, then to a car, then a limousine, then a helicopter! There is no end to temptation.

Your mental desires or temptation should be kept under control to stop this chain reaction which finally leads to disaster. When you reach the ultimate stage of control of your mind temptation does not get generated at all. But that is one in a million cases. Ordinary human beings should recognise and understand the reality and adjust themselves with it as early as possible instead of building castles in the air. Do not increase your needs unnecessarily and disturb your balance of mind, happiness, pleasantness and peace.

Always remember the equation-

$$\text{Happiness} = \frac{1}{\text{Expectation}}$$

1.10.3 *Greed or desire of senses-*

Desires are everlasting. Once a desire is satisfied, the next one follows. Like waves of the sea they are unending.

Desire is sensation with the object of its attainment.

Desire is never extinguished by enjoyment of desired object, it only grows stronger.

If a sensation is pleasurable we want to attain it. When one is bored with one form of pleasure another form of pleasure is sought after, with a new idea, new symbol, new significance, with new experience which is more satisfying. The whole process of stimulation, sensation, perception and desire is continuously changing around the centre "me." One should passively observe the cravings, longings, ambitions, aspiration to enable to control them.

Human beings have 5 senses- sense of touch, sight, taste, hearing and smell which the mind notices through the inputs received from skin, eyes, tongue, ears and nose respectively.

Ego forces us not only to crave for the best but always generates the feeling of "better than others". We crave for the best food and drinks to satisfy our taste. We aspire for the best perfumes and scents. We long for smooth and velvety touch. We are mad after listening to a variety in music-vocal and instrumental. We love to feast our eyes with the picturesque sites at hill-stations and beaches. We love to look at the beauty of persons, of paintings and of nature. Human beings are continuously restless to meet the needs of ego and long for better and better ways to satisfy the senses.

Suppose you desire to eat a cake. How much will you eat? Cakes for breakfast, cakes for lunch, cakes for evening snacks, cakes for dinner! Will it be pleasurable? Will it satisfy you? If you are offered cakes from breakfast to dinner even for a day, you will not only dislike eating it but you would be even fed up by its sight!

Will this end your craving for food? Not at all! You would be after some other food. In short, you are never satisfied; you never get gratification but you certainly notice that the craving for food is short-lived.

If you restrain and control your mind, then you can be free of the unending desires of the senses.

1.10.4 *Anger-*

Anger originates from unfulfilled desire. Every human being has desire for property, for position, for power, for comfort, to be loved etc.

Thus anger begins a chain reaction and the explosion results in surfacing of a number of vices. To avoid this, anger must be controlled. Anger should be controlled by an antidote of calmness. Time is the best remedy to control anger. You slowly count 1 to 10 or even 1 to 100. You will find anger has reduced considerably. If you get angry at 8 O'clock and can control your mind up to 8.15 the anger will totally die down. You may practice meditation to control anger.

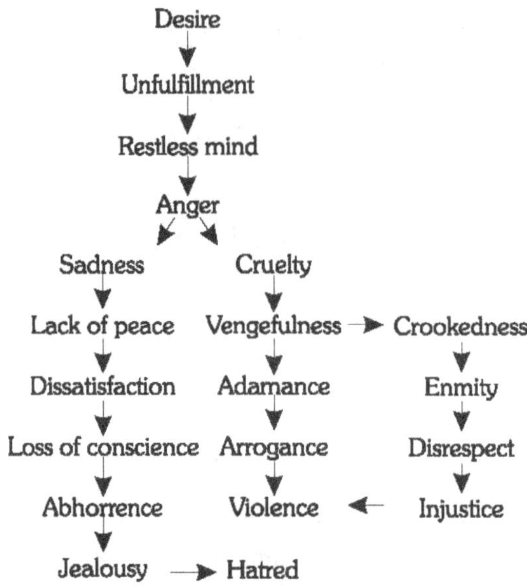

1.10.5 *Arrogance / Adamance-*

Ego- the vice part of the basic logic Ego- breeds arrogance and adamance. "I am the wisest, I am the cleverest, I am the most brilliant, I am the most powerful, and I am the richest. No body can come anywhere close to me." These misunderstandings breed arrogance and adamance. We forget that just as we have ego, others as well have their egos. We create enmity by our arrogance. We create emotions of hatred, abhorrence, disrespect and revenge in the minds of others. Finally when one loses his power, position, authority, money, youthfulness and energy one becomes helpless. One repents. One is ashamed of his deeds. But then it is too late.

There is no person ever born in this world who gained by his arrogance and adamance any benefit whatsoever, leave aside getting happiness, pleasure, peace and satisfaction. Then why display these vices of arrogance and adamance? Do you think that others will insult you or value you less if you are not arrogant and adamant? Do you think your lenience and modesty will lead to disrespect towards you? Do you equate courtesy with sycophancy and arrogance with self- respect? You never get disrespected or insulted if you do not insult others.

Let us not get disgusted or disheartened by defeats. Let us not allow success to develop into arrogance and adamance.

1.10.6 *Jealousy / Envy / Abhorrence / Hatred-*

All these vices arise from unfulfilled desires and lack of affection and respect.

Envy- originates from desire. When do you envy a person? If property, or position, or power, or popularity of another person are desired by you and if there is at least a remote chance for you to get it then you envy him or her e.g. If you are a municipal corporator and some one gets elected as mayor, you may envy him. But when you are a corporator you just do not envy some one getting elected as the President of USA, since there is not the remotest chance of your getting elected anywhere there! And after all how long you will keep on envying your mayor colleague? Till you get accustomed to it within a week or two. If you really love and respect your mayor friend you will never envy him!

Thus, you envy a person when-

  (i)   he is slightly superior to you and in possession of power,
 (ii)   you have a very thin chance to become the same
(iii)   you do not have affection and respect for that person.

It can also be observed that 'envy' is an emotion which is very short lived.

Hatred- arises from strong dislikes. Normally you are in a better position than the person you hate. The primary logic of ego and desire to live develops your secondary logic of beliefs, understanding, concepts likes, dislikes etc. You form your own opinions. You form your own values. You hate theft and hence who steals. You hate a person who tells lies. You hate hypocrites. You hate sycophants. You even hate dirty, filthy, shabby people. As a result you start hating poverty, you start hating the downtrodden.

If you develop virtues like kindness, sympathy, compassion, love, affection, respect and forgiveness and you can keep aside pride and prejudice, you can control the emotion of hate and avoid it.

"Hate the sin and not the sinner" attitude should be developed to enable one to repent for his mistakes and improve himself.

Jealousy- Normally jealousy is generated amongst people of equal status or level. When a person claims to be superior than the other, jealousy is generated.

Abhorrence- is an emotion which can be considered as a combination of jealousy, envy and hatred. All these emotions should be superseded and controlled by thought, by conscience, by a balanced and peaceful mind. To live a healthy life these emotions must be carefully dealt with, otherwise they may destroy our professional, family or social life.

If we develop compassion and kindness, get rid of pride and prejudice, control our mind to avoid emotions superseding thought, as a result envy, jealousy, hatred and abhorrence will be totally eliminated from our mind.

1.11 SELF AWARENESS-

Life is a relationship of an individual with the world around him- of humans, animals, plants, buildings, roads, towns, nations and everything. Awareness is to know these relations "as they are" in reality.

To be aware one must experience the world around passively. The entire process of mind- stimulation by surroundings, sensation through the five senses, identification and response in terms of behaviour, thought and emotion - should be observed passively.

Passivity is not idleness, not sleep but extreme alertness. You watch without enquiry, without justification, without response, without judgement as good or bad, without condemnation, without questioning, without speculating.

It is an impartial perception where there is neither attachment nor queries; neither pleasure nor displeasure. Impartial perception is strictly concerned with the phenomenon of the present; it is neither memory of the past nor imagination of the future. Whatever is happening at the present moment of perception must necessarily be reality. Equanimity and impartiality are synonymous with passive observation.

Never react when you are under control of emotions- sad,

glad, and mad- whatever they may be. Act only when emotions die down. Then you act without pride, without prejudice, without expectation and without fear.

In short-

(1) The "breath" which accompanies us from birth to death is the medium which easily and effectively establishes contact with the mind. By carefully and passively observing breath we reach the mind.

(2) The body responses are a reflection of the mind. The moment you are scared, your breathing rate increases, your heartbeats are faster, your blood pressure increases, your mouth feels dry, and you may even perspire. The effect of your mind and its emotions on your body has to be observed passively. This is the first step.

(3) To know that these responses or changes in body functioning are temporary is the second stage. e.g. If you are sad or glad because of some incident like winning or losing a match it may last for a few seconds, or a few minutes or a few hours and not for weeks, months, years or a lifetime.

(4) To know that the body responses are due to memory or previous experience is the third step. e.g. If A is beating B and C intervenes then the moment C meets them subsequently-

- A would generate a feeling of revenge or hatred
- B would generate a feeling of gratitude and affection.

Thus meeting the same person 'C' at the same time generated different feeling in the mind of A and B due to the memory of previous experience.

(5) To learn to dissociate the previous experience or 'prejudice' from memory to eliminate the cause of sorrow is the 4th step which is not only the most important but also the most difficult to follow.

(6) The final step is to achieve the state of the mind of "awareness" as "enlightened" where you learn to accept the realities of life, as they are without enslaving emotions. Then you control your desires, ego and achieve a state of "liberated mind" or "self-awareness" or "self realization" or self enlightenment" whatever you would like to call it.

(7) By controlling the normal breathing rhythm of 18 breaths per minute one can control the explosion of emotions.

1.12 MEDITATION-

To purify the mind, to give it rest and freshness and to exercise the mind to keep it fit, meditation is essential.

When the output of the mind tends towards zero and one concentrates on one of the five senses or breathing, the act is called as meditation. During meditation talking, reading, writing, thinking, movements, expression of the emotions is brought to almost zero level. Meditation can mainly be done in 6 ways.

(i) By concentrating only on the sense of sight. A candle or a small bright spot is created- preferably a point source- and the entire attention are concentrated on to this bright spot. This normally requires dark surroundings.

(ii) By concentrating only on the sense of hearing. A deep ringing sound like "Oooo...um" is created by oneself or by using a musical / sound system and the entire attention is concentrated on this sound. You need silence around.

(iii) By concentrating only on the sense of taste. You can keep a grape or a piece of an apple in your mouth and concentrate on the taste for 30 minutes.

(iv) By concentrating on the sense of smell. By burning a scented stick or by spraying a scent in a closed room one can concentrate on the sense of smell.

(v) By concentrating on the sense of "feel" or touch. From head to feet each and every limb is passively observed for sense of feel- pressure, temperature, wetness, numbness, itching etc. Since the entire body from feet to head is involved in this meditation it is the most effective. This is also called as "vipassana" or "Preksha-Dhyan" or "Shareer preksha".

(vi) By concentrating on breath which accompanies one from birth to death. This can be done any time, anywhere and easily. When the mind is in the grip of lust, temptation, anger, desire, jealousy, hatred, abhorrence, tensions, worries then the breathing rate increases, blood pressure rises, hormonal and digestive secretions are affected. By passively observing breathing, breathing rate can be regulated and all other things like blood pressure, acidity, digestive and hormonal secretions are restored to normalcy.

"Samadhi" is the ultimate stage in meditation when both the input and output of the mind are at zero level. During this stage the intelligence is at work with only interaction between memory and logic without any interference from the input of five senses or output of five attitudes. This enables generations of creative thoughts, important inventions and discovery taking place during *"Samadhi"* state of mind and some feel that they get "divine message"!

Meditation needs-

(i)   Stillness

(ii) Solitude

(iii) Silence

(iv) Freedom from fear.

Every day spending at least 15 to 30 minutes in meditation results in-

(i)   Rest to the mind

(ii) Increase in concentration

(iii) Balanced mind

(iv) Equanimity

(v)   Firmness and determination

(vi) Better grasping

(vii) Sharpened intelligence

(viii) Decisiveness

(ix) Calmness

(x)   Freedom from worries, tensions, fear etc.

(xi) Help for achieving freedom from lust, anger, desire, temptation, arrogance, adamance, hatred, abhorrence and jealousy etc.

(xii) Digestive and hormonal secretions are improved.

(xiii) Mind is purified.

1.13 PHYSICAL HEALTH-

Physical health is dependent on mental condition. Conversely "Sound body sound mind" principle also applies.

To keep healthy there has to be an appropriate balance between food, exercise, rest, work and study. Every individual has different needs and a different physical and mental set up. The needs of people in cold and tropical countries, of the old and the young, of those doing heavy physical labour and those having table work would vary.

Excess of anything- food, rest, work or exercise should be avoided. Food to suit one's calorie requirement, minimum 30 minutes of exercise every day, 8 hours of work daily and 7 hours of sleep every day are essential. Cleanliness of body is also extremely important.

Great minds discuss ideas,
Average minds discuss events,
Small minds discuss people.

Umbutu

Umbutu is African culture to express reciprocity, dignity, harmony and humanity in the interest of building and maintaining community with justice and mutual caring.

"I am because we are."
An Anthropologist kept a box of sweets near a tree and asked a group of children to run 50 meters and grab th sweets. Whosoever reaches first will have all the sweets.

The entire group of children held each other's hand and ran together to the sweet box.All shared the sweets equally and enjoyed.
When asked by anthropologist as to why they did so, they replied in unison,"UMBUTU".

How all of us can be happy, when only one gets the sweets and others don't? We are happy when all get sweets. "I am because we are."

2 PRINCIPLES OF HUMANITY

2.1 NEED FOR PRINCIPLES OF HUMANITY

The first and foremost requirement of humans is SAFETY, that is human being must survive .What should be done to have safety?

- A human should not kill a human
- Human should be protected from animals that can kill human
- Human should be protected from life threatening diseases
- Human should get its basic needs for survival-
  Clean air to breath
  Contamination free mineral water to drink
  Food to meet his requirements of 1500 to 3500 calories/day
  Clothes to protect from weather and to maintain needs of society
  Shelter to protect from weather

If safety is ensured but life is full of quarrels, disputes, fights, then the life will become unbearable. PEACE is the next requirement of human society. What should be done to have peace?

Human should develop mutual trust, understanding and goodwill to eliminate hatred, animosity and belligerent attitude and be tolerant and restrained. There is no "GOOD" war and there is no "BAD" peace.

If, SAFETY and PEACE are ensured, but it is a graveyard peace—everyone is serious, pensive, sad, depressed –will it be OK? No. So the next requirement is HAPPINESS. Learn to enjoy your work, without expectations, and be happy and try to make others happy.

Happiness is temporary but satisfaction and CONTENTMENT are permanent.

Thus SAFETY, PEACE, HAPPINESS, and CONTENTMENT are four basic requirements of human beings.

A human being, on birth starts getting to know the world around. His parents, siblings, relations, neighbours, pets, birds flying around, plants and trees are his first acquaintances .As the child grows, he gets to know more and more people, animals, birds, plants. He develops relations with inanimate objects like his toys, his tricycle, his home, houses and roads around his home, his school. The process continues through out his life.

Human beings need some guiding principles for peaceful co-existence with other living and non living object during course of their life. These are Principles of Humanity.

Principles of Humanity give us scientific, logical and global principles which when imbibed, inculcated or used for 'programming' or 'conditioning' (sanskar) of the mind will result in development of virtues, elimination of vices and consequently human life would be safe, peaceful, happy and contented.

These principles can be broadly catagorised as

Human Ethics:- The laws of Morality that are globally acceptable, like laws of science.

Human Duties:- People are aware of Human Rights but rights and duties go hand in hand and duties come first.

Human Rights:- These are declared by United Nations Organistion in 1948.

These three categories overlap each other.

Humanity is the quality, character, nature that makes us human. It is "Oneness Of Mankind" on this planet. It is brotherly love, fellow feeling, kindness, compassion, altruism, benevolence, and desire to help between humans.

2.2 PRINCIPLES OF HUMANITY-

HUMAN ETHICS

2.2.1 Truth, Non-violence, Love, Compassion, Forgiveness, Peace, Liberty, Equality, Fraternity, Respect, Tolerance, Restraint, Patience, Altruism, Benevolence and Justice should be adhered to as values of life.

2.2.2 Eliminate the vices ego, lust, desire, temptation, jealousy, hatred, envy, arrogance, adamance, anger, cruelty, vengeance, ostentation, hypocrisy, flattery, sycophancy, nepotism and ill feeling.

2.2.3 Building of a society free from corruption, adultery, gambling, addiction, atrocities, oppression, terrorism and exploitation, should begin from ourselves.

2.2.4 Destructive, terrorist, heinous, hideous and shameful acts should not be carried out.

2.2.5 Diligence, sincerity, integrity, honesty, discipline, dedication, devotion and determination have no substitute. Have enthusiasm. Avoid boredom, laziness.

2.2.6 Always follow righteous way. The motive behind an action and its effect on individual, society and mankind will enable us to decide, the righteous way.

2.2.7 Develop virtues and eliminate vices.

2.2.8 Live life with dignity, decency and decorum; with openness and transparency; with accountability and responsiveness; with simplicity and modesty.

HUMAN DUTIES

2.2.9 Only truthful, scientific, logical and global principles should be adhered to. Every effect has a cause. Everything happens as per laws of nature. Laws of nature, is science. Some laws of nature are known to us some are unknown. Human should strive to know the unknown laws of nature.

2.2.10 Control of human population, ecological balance, pollution of air and noise, contamination of water, adulteration of food and drugs are major problems of human beings in the 21st century. Every human being should strive to solve these problems- at various levels- individually, with the help of their families as well as at social, political, administrative and judicial levels. Flora and Fauna must be protected to maintain ecological balance.

2.2.11 Never react under control of emotions, wait till emotions die down, and act with deep thinking.

2.2.12 Every human being should work for development, progress and improvement of mankind.

2.2.13 Constructive, Creative work that would bring people together should be done.

2.2.14 Be optimistic. Never be pessimistic. Plan for the worst but hope for the best. Accept the reality.

2.2.15 Sports and sportsmanship should be encouraged and patronised.

2.2.16 Art should be encouraged and patronised.

2.2.17 Organisations for blind, deaf, dumb, mentally and physically handicapped, hospitals, orphanages should be patronised. Spend at least 1% of your earnings for charity.

2.2.18 Every physically and mentally fit human in age group of 20 to 60 (+/-5)years should try to earn his living without causing harm or injustice to others. Do not earn by theft, dacoit, fraud, corruption, extortion. Honorary work to look after family or society is as good as earning. Avoid child labour.

2.2.19 Try to develop alert, balanced, stable and decisive mind.

Balanced mind means equanimity. It keeps away personal likes/dislikes, pleasures/pains, honours/insults, praise/ridicule, pride/prejudice and is impartial.

Stable mind is one that does not yield to pressures, threats, fear, greed, obligations and expectations. It is steadfastness.

Decisive mind is free from doubts—to be or not to be-. It can discern between truth or untruth, just or unjust, right or wrong, acceptable or un-acceptable, proper or improper.

2.2.20 Let us make this planet a better place to live.

HUMAN RIGHTS

2.2.21 Universal declaration of human rights adopted and proclaimed on 10ᵗʰ Dec. 1948 by the General Assembly of United Nations must be strictly adhered to.

UNIVERSAL DECLARATION OF HUMAN RIGHTS

On December 10, 1948 the General Assembly of the United Nations adopted and proclaimed the Universal Declaration of Human Rights the full text of which appears in the following pages. Following this historic act the Assembly called upon all Member countries to publicize the text of the Declaration and "to cause it to be disseminated, displayed, read and expounded principally in schools and other educational institutions, without distinction based on the political status of countries or territories."

PREAMBLE

Whereas recognition of the inherent dignity and of the equal and inalienable rights of all members of the human family is the foundation of freedom, justice and peace in the world.

Whereas disregard and contempt for human rights have resulted in barbarous acts which have outraged the conscience of mankind, and the advent of a world in which human beings shall enjoy freedom of speech and belief and freedom from fear and want has been proclaimed as the highest aspiration of the common people.

Whereas it is essential, if man is not to be compelled to have recourse, as a last resort, to rebellion against tyranny and oppression, that human rights should be protected by the rule of law.

Whereas it is essential to promote the development of friendly relations between nations.

Whereas the peoples of the United Nations have in the Charter reaffirmed their faith in fundamental human rights, in the dignity and worth of the human person and in the equal rights of men and women and have determined to promote social progress and better standards of life in larger freedom. Whereas Member States have pledged themselves to achieve, in co-operation with the United Nations, the promotion of universal respect for and observance of human rights and fundamental freedoms.

Whereas a common understanding of these rights and freedoms is of the greatest importance for the full realization of this pledge.

Now, Therefore THE GENERAL ASSEMBLY proclaims THIS UNIVERSAL DECLARATION OF HUMAN RIGHTS as a common standard of achievement for all peoples and all nations, to the end that every individual and every organ of society, keeping this Declaration constantly in mind, shall strive by teaching and education to promote respect for these rights and freedoms and by progressive measures, national and international, to secure their universal and effective recognition and observance, both among the people of Member States themselves and among the peoples of territories under their jurisdiction.

ARTICLE 1

- All human beings are born free and equal in dignity and rights.

They are endowed with reason and conscience and should act towards one another in a spirit of brotherhood.

ARTICLE 2

- Everyone is entitled to all the rights and freedoms set forth in this Declaration, without distinction of any kind, such as race, colour, sex, language, religion, political or other opinion, national or social origin, property, birth or other status. Furthermore, no distinction shall be made on the basis of the political, jurisdictional or international status of the country or territory to which a person belongs, whether it is independent, trust, non-self-governing or under any other limitation of sovereignty.

ARTICLE 3

- Everyone has the right to life, liberty and security of person.

ARTICLE 4

- No one shall be held in slavery or servitude; slavery and the slave trade shall be prohibited in all their forms.

ARTICLE 5

- No one shall be subjected to torture or to cruel, inhuman or degrading treatment of punishment.

ARTICLE 6

- Everyone has the right to recognition everywhere as a person before the law.

ARTICLE 7

- All are equal before the law and are entitled without any discrimination to equal protection of the law. All are entitled to equal protection against any discrimination in violation of this Declaration and against any incitement to such discrimination.

ARTICLE 8

- Everyone has the right to an effective remedy by the competent national tribunals for acts violating the fundamental rights granted him by the constitution or by law.

ARTICLE 9

- No one shall be subjected to arbitrary arrest, detention or exile.

ARTICLE 10

- Everyone is entitled in full equality to a fair and public hearing by an independent and impartial tribunal, in the determination of his rights and obligations and of any criminal charge against him.

ARTICLE 11

- (1) Everyone charged with a penal offence has the right to be presumed innocent until proved guilty according to law in a public trial at which he has had all the guarantees necessary for his defence.
- (2) No one shall be held guilty of any penal offence on account of any act or omission which did not constitute a penal offence, under national or international law, at the time when it was committed. Nor shall a heavier penalty be imposed than the one that was applicable at the time the penal offence was committed.

ARTICLE 12

- No one shall be subjected to arbitrary interference with his privacy, family, home or correspondence, nor to attacks upon his honour and reputation. Everyone has the right to the protection of the law against such interference or attacks.

ARTICLE 13

- (1) everyone has the right to freedom of movement and residence within the borders of each state.
- (2) Everyone has the right to leave any country, including his own, and to return to his country.

ARTICLE 14

- (1) everyone has the right to seek and to enjoy in other countries asylum from persecution.
- (2) This right may not be invoked in the case of prosecutions genuinely arising from non-political crimes or from acts contrary to the purposes and principles of the United Nations.

ARTICLE 15

- (1) everyone has the right to a nationality.
- (2) No one shall be arbitrarily deprived of his nationality nor denied the right to change his nationality.

ARTICLE 16

- (1) Men and women of full age, without any limitation due to race, nationality or religion, have the right to marry and to found a family. They are entitled to equal rights as to marriage and at its dissolution.
- (2) Marriage shall be entered into only with the free and full consent of the intending spouses.
- (3) The family is the natural and fundamental group unit of society and is entitled to protection by society and the State.

ARTICLE 17

- (1) everyone has the right to own property alone as well as in association with others.
- (2) No one shall be arbitrarily deprived of his property.

ARTICLE 18

- Everyone has the right to freedom of thought, conscience and religion; this right includes freedom to change his religion or belief, and freedom, either alone or in community with others and in public or private, to manifest his religion or belief in teaching, practice, worship and observance.

ARTICLE 19

- Everyone has the right to freedom of thought, conscience and religion; this right includes freedom to hold opinions without interference and to seek, receive and impart information and ideas through any media and regardless of frontiers.

ARTICLE 20

- (1) everyone has the right to freedom of peaceful assembly and association.
- (2) No one may be compelled to belong to an association.

ARTICLE 21

- (1) Everyone has the right to take part in the government of his country, directly or through freely chosen representatives.
- (2) Everyone has the right of equal access to public service in his country.
- (3) The will of the people shall be the basis of the authority of government; this will shall be expressed in periodic and genuine elections which shall be by universal and equal suffrage and shall be held by secret vote or by equivalent free voting procedure.

ARTICLE 22

- Everyone, as a member of society, has the right to social security and is entitled to realization, through national effort and international co-operation and in accordance with the organization and resources of each State, of the economic, social and cultural rights indispensable for his dignity and the free development of his personality.

ARTICLE 23

- (1) Everyone has the right to work, to free choice of employment, to just and favourable conditions of work and to protection against unemployment.
- (2) Everyone, without any discrimination, has the right to equal pay for equal work.
- (3) Everyone who works has the right to just and favourable remuneration ensuring for himself and his family an existence worthy of human dignity, and supplemented, if necessary, by other means of social protection.
- (4) Everyone has right to form and to join trade unions for the protection of his interests.

ARTICLE 24

- Everyone has the right to rest and leisure, including reasonable limitation of working hours and periodic holidays with pay.

ARTICLE 25

- (1) Everyone has the right to a standard of living adequate for the health and well-being of himself and of his family, including food, clothing, housing and medical care and

necessary social services, and the right to security in the event of unemployment, sickness, disability, widowhood, old age or other lack of livelihood in circumstances beyond his control.
- (2) Motherhood and childhood are entitled to special care and assistance. All children, whether born in or out of wedlock, shall enjoy the same social protection.

ARTICLE 26

- (1) Everyone has the right to education. Education shall be free, at least in the elementary and fundamental stages. Elementary education shall be compulsory. Technical and professional education shall be made generally available and higher education shall be equally accessible to all on the basis of merit.
- (2) Education shall be directed to the full development of the human personality and to the strengthening of respect for human rights and fundamental freedoms. It shall promote understanding, tolerance and friendship among all nations, racial or religious groups, and shall further the activities of the United Nations for the maintenance of peace.
- (3) Parents have a prior right to choose the kind of education that shall be given to their children.

ARTICLE 27

- (1) Everyone has the right freely to participate in the cultural life of the community, to enjoy the arts and to share in scientific advancement and its benefits.
- (2) Everyone has the right to the protection of the moral and material interests resulting from any scientific, literary or artistic production of which he is the author.

ARTICLE 28

- Everyone is entitled to a social and international order in which the rights and freedoms set forth in this Declaration can be fully realized.

ARTICLE 29

- (1) everyone has duties to the community in which alone the free and full development of his personality is possible.

- (2) In the exercise of his rights and freedoms, everyone shall be subject only to such limitations as are determined by law solely for the purpose of securing due recognition and respect for the rights and freedoms of others and of meeting the just requirements of morality, public order and the general welfare in a democratic society.
- (3) These rights and freedoms may in no case be exercised contrary to the purposes and principles of the United Nations.

ARTICLE 30

- Nothing in this Declaration may be interpreted as implying for any State, group or person any right to engage in any activity or to perform any act aimed at the destruction of any of the rights and freedoms set forth herein.

2.3 HUMAN CULTURE

Culture represents customs and traditions of a large group of people at a particular place, at a particular time period. It includes dance, music, costumes/dresses, sports, festivals, daily routines. It varies from place to place as well as at the same place from time to time. It is influenced by local and religious beliefs, current trends in social and political atmosphere. Manners and etiquettes are influenced by culture and hence culture is some times related to ethics. Diversity of culture is inherent. Appreciation of other's culture as well picking up something from other's culture is a continuous process. Unity of mankind with diverse cultures is the need of the hour and is met with by coming together under umbrella of Humanity.

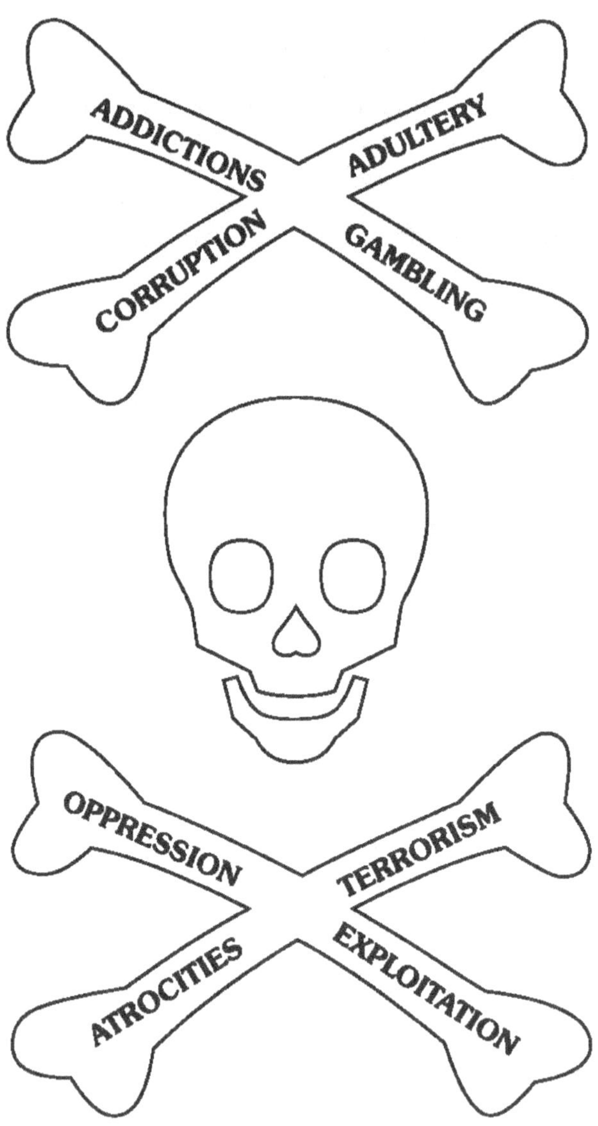

DANGERS TO HUMANITY

3 GOD, REBIRTH, SOUL, GHOST ETC.

3.1 HISTORY OF CONCEPT OF GOD-

Thousands of years back primitive, ignorant human being, staying in caves, was in terrific panic due to deafening sound of thunderstorm and ear piercing sound of lightening pervading entire sky. He concluded that there is a tremendously powerful entity with whom he can not fight nor can he run away. He has to surrender to this great power in the sky. He has to please it and solicit its protection. Thus, the concept of God in the sky was born.

Even after learning what thunderstorm and lightening are and how they get generated, the mankind is reluctant to leave the concept of God and his abode heaven in the sky.

It can be noticed from the history of mankind for the last 10,000 years that the concept of god, heaven, satan, hell, ghost, soul, rebirth were created by imagination and fantasies to reveal the mysteries of universe. Once these virtual and mysterious creatures were created by mankind, their habitats, their size, their shape, their nature, their likes and dislikes were also attributed. Also various ways of worshipping, offering and sacrifices for these imaginary creatures were devised to please them and to avoid their anger and vengeance. Mankind did not stop at this but it was propagated that the factual world or the world in reality is imaginary and the virtual world of gods, ghosts heaven and hell is actually the real one. It is very unfortunate that even today majority of religions propagate this idea and there are millions who follow it!

Small pox, which was a deadly disease was considered a vengeance of a goddess till it was established that it was caused by germs. Now that the treatment is available and small pox has been eradicated, the need of pleasing the goddess is eliminated. Imagine how foolish and ridiculous it was to worship a goddess, to offer her food and sacrifice animals to get rid of small pox!

It can be inferred that wherever real cause of effect is

unknown the concept of 'God' and 'Ghost' helped mankind to offer an explanation. The moment the real cause is revealed the 'god' or 'ghost' gets eliminated. Thus through education only these misconception would be removed.

God is the greatest creation of man! There are a lot of unanswered questions, such as-

How was this universe created?

What was the past of it?

What would happen in future?

What are the mysteries of birth and death?

and so on.

The creation of the concept of 'God' enabled man to answer these questions. 'God' the creator has created this world was the answer and 'God' the destroyer destroys it.

The two major views expressed by believers are pantheism-everything is god and god is everything and agnosticism- nothing is and can be known of god.

3.2 CONCEPT OF REBIRTH, SOUL, HEAVEN, HELL AND GHOST-

Why then did the so called omnipotent, omnipresent 'God' create such a world full of suffering, oppression, crime, terrorism and so many vices? The concept of "rebirth" was created to answer this query. Sufferings are result of sins of the 'previous birth', was the answer.

If there is "rebirth" then there has to be an entity which does not get destroyed and takes 'rebirth' and the concept of "soul" was born.

If you perform well, your deeds are good in the previous birth then this 'soul' will take rebirth of a "happy" animal and you will reach such a fine place called "Heaven" where there is no sorrow, no shortages, no scarcity. It is only plenty, happiness, joy and fun in 'Heaven', "up above".

If you sin, you will be thrown into "hell" "down below" where 'satan' will harass you and you will take birth in a lower category. Unsatisfied souls roam around as ghosts in the form of previous birth.

Thus all the imaginary concepts of God, rebirth, soul, ghost, heaven, hell and satan were created by man.

Considering today's knowledge of mankind about outer space and of the earth, no sensible and educated human being would believe in the concepts of "Heaven" up above in the sky and "Hell" down below.

After dedicated and devoted work of Dr. Kovoor of Sri Lanka and many others the non existence of ghosts has now been finally established.

Now let us take an example to examine the concept of "rebirth" based on previous good deeds or sins by considering its application to the non-living, only for the purpose of clarification and understanding.

A heap of iron ore was divided into 4 different parts and converted into metal.

(i) The first part was converted into a spoon, which was used by a beautiful Hollywood actress!

(ii) The second part was converted into a knife, which went to a butcher to kill animals and take away their lives!

(iii) The third part went to a surgeon as a knife to save lives of many!

(iv) The fourth part was converted into a sanitary fitting to drain off excreta!

Now do you attribute these drastically different statuses of the four parts originating from the same iron ore due to their previous birth?

Plants are also living things. What about their rebirth?

Can you imagine how various animals, mosquitoes, microscopic and submicroscopic germs etc. should behave to get a better life during the "next" birth?

Most of us, particularly the civilised and the educated have come to a stage to accept that ghost, rebirth, heaven, hell, satan are all imaginary concepts far from reality.

People have serious doubts about the existence of 'soul' and quite a few of them have come to a stage to believe that it does not exist in reality. However, continuous hammering for over 5000 years has had its effect and even those who firmly believe in non existence of the soul innocently send a message of "May his soul rest in peace"!

Still it will be extremely difficult for the mankind to understand and accept the fact that 'God' is an imaginary concept due to continuous hammering of this concept on the mankind for over 5000 years!

3.3 PRESENT CONCEPT OF GOD-

3.3.1 God as a creator- It is believed that the entire universe is created by God. In fact the letter 'G' in the word God stands for "Generation".

The law of nature states nothing can be created and or destroyed. Since there is no creation, there is no creator. There is continuous conversion of mass and energy from one form to another.

Tremendous energy is created inside the sun due to atomic fusion. Similarly tremendous energy due to atomic fission is generated in all atomic power plants. Thus fusion and fission or association and dissociation or synthesis and division is the process of nature.

A small seed grows into a big tree which in turn produces a small seed with an inherent property to create a similar big tree. Thus, there is continuous expansion and contraction and there are so many permutations and combinations in these processes which lead to an infinitely variable species in animal and plant kingdom as well as a very wide variety of inanimate matter.

The truth is, it is neither essential nor necessary to have a creator but the entire universe runs according to the laws of nature and properties of matter. The concept of God as a creator therefore holds no good.

3.3.2 God as rewarder- It is believed that God rewards good people. Hence every effort is made to please "the God".

If you look around, you will find a number of deserving people not getting their due rewards in spite of their faith in God and the service rendered by them to please Him. The moment one gets poor rewards the reasons are found to absolve Him. Also reward to other animals and plants are never explained.

The truth is that God itself is an imaginary concept and reward

by God is an impossibility.

3.3.3 God as a provider- It is believed that all our needs are provided by God. Food, shelter, clothes, comforts, happiness, wealth and health.

If you carefully study the history of mankind you will notice that man has developed the art of growing crops, building his own shelter, building wells and dams to get water and so on. You have to provide for yourself- that is the truth.

Every year 20 million human beings die of starvation. There is also no account of other animals dieing for want of food or water.

3.3.4 Vengeance of God- Stories with dreadful consequences in various mythologies are full of descriptions of vengeance of God. Till a couple of centuries ago even lightning, cyclones, earthquakes, famines, diseases like small pox were considered a vengeance of God. Now all of us know the truth! Worshiping, surrendering, giving offerings and sacrificing animals and even human beings as in the past to avoid vengeance of God is therefore irrelevant.

3.3.5 God as a protector- It was believed that God protects from calamities, diseases, evils and demons etc. What was the protection that was offered to millions who died in wars? What was the protection offered to millions getting killed by plague, malaria, small pox, typhoid and other epidemics? Millions get affected by cyclones, earthquakes and other natural calamities what is the protection offered? The fact is man devised his own remedies to protect himself.

3.3.6 God the controller- It is believed that the God is omnipresent, omnipotent, omniscient and has a total control over happenings in the universe. This world is full of crime, terrorism, violence, massacres, heinous and hideous acts and there is no one controlling!

3.3.7 God as a means to express respect, faith and devotion- The concept of God provides people an acceptable idol to express their faith and devotion. People do not feel shy to accept their mistakes and misdeeds in front of God. The concept of God provides them with an entity to pay respect without disturbing their ego. As a person grows in stature his ego expands. Heads of state, chiefs of multinational companies, film stars, industrialists, political / social / religious leaders have very high egos. They are always in search of God or Godmen to confess their mistakes and misdeeds to open out their minds, express their repentance and vow their loyalties.

A suitable practical alternative is to treat the 'Sun' as a god for this purpose as explained in 3.4.

There is therefore, no one who creates. There is no one who provides, protects, rewards or blesses.

God is an imaginary concept like other imaginary concepts of ghost, heaven, hell, satan, soul and rebirth. It is not easy to assimilate this fact due to continuous hammering of these imaginary concepts for over 5000 years.

There are several religions like Buddhism, Jainism which do not believe in concept of God. Kapil and Charvak the Hindu philosophers did not believe in the concept of God.

3.4 SUN AS A SUBSTITUTE FOR CONCEPT OF GOD-

It would create a void unless an adequate substitute is provided for the concept of God at least as an interim measure.

Some people need God to worship, to pray, to seek blessings, to express respect. Can there be such a God which meets the conditions of being scientific, logical and global? Can there be such a God, who is a reality and not an imagination? Can there be a God without association of superstition and blind faith?

Yes, such a stature is possessed by the 'Sun'. The Sun is the source of all life and energy on the earth. Without the Sun there would be no life. The Sun is the prime source of energy- light and heat. Wind and tidal energies have there origin in the Sun. The basis of measurement of time is associated with the Sun- one year is the time required by the earth to complete one rotation around the Sun. Plants generate food from solar energy and serve as food to animals including human beings, thus Sun gives us food.

Let us therefore, worship our source of life, our source of energy, our source of food, our reference of time. It's existence is an absolute reality. Every one can see it. Even blind can feel its warmth. All religions worship it. It is globally worshiped from Japan in the far east to Inkas of South America in the far west!

One should not forget that there is no God and to consider the Sun as God is only an intermediate step from falsehood of the concept of God to the reality that there is no God.

3.5 CONCLUSIONS-

Most of the people in a society tend to believe that whatever is traditional and conventional and whatever is postulated by the saints or the Holy people or some scriptures is the truth, is correct, is right and is the reality. Certain customs conventions, sayings or scriptures are respected, accepted, practised and advocated by blind faith only. These autocratic tendencies in the intellectual field tend to defeat reason and logic and leads to intellectual dishonesty. It hinders dynamism and progress of mankind. For the benefit of mankind one must follow the path of strong reasoning, logic and analysis to establish the rule of conscience.

Unless the mankind comes out of the imaginary fear of vengeance of the God, imaginary banes and boons of God, unreal concepts of life after death, there would be no peace and happiness. To achieve the goal of developing benevolent individual with high moral standards and to create society with good behaviour and good thoughts the concepts of heaven and hell, of rewards and punishment by God are not at all necessary.

MONKEYS

Start with a cage containing five monkeys. Inside the cage, hang a banana on a string and place a set of stairs under it. Before long, a monkey will go to the stairs and start to climb towards the banana. As soon as he touches the stairs, spray all of the other monkeys with cold water. After a while, another monkey makes an attempt with the same result- all the other monkeys are sprayed with cold water. Pretty soon, when another monkey tries to climb the stairs, the other monkeys will try to prevent it.

Now, put away the cold water. Remove one monkey from the cage and replace it with a new one. The new monkey sees the banana and wants to climb the stairs. To his surprise and horror, all of the other monkeys attack him. After another attempt and attack, he knows that if he tries to climb the stairs, he will be assaulted.

Next, remove another of the original five monkeys and replace it with a new one. The newcomer goes to the stairs and is attacked. The previous newcomer takes part in the punishment with enthusiasm! Likewise, replace a third original monkey with a new one, then a fourth, then the fifth. Every time the newest monkey takes to the stairs, he is attacked. Most of the monkeys that are beating him have no idea why they were not permitted to climb the stairs or why they are participating in the beating of the newest monkey. After replacing all the original monkeys, none of the remaining monkeys have ever been sprayed with cold water. Nevertheless, no monkey ever again approaches the stairs to try for the banana. Why not?

Because as far as they know that's the way it's always been done around here.

This also says a lot about us human-beings too...

We follow Religion, customs and traditions exactly in the same manner, without even thinking once, that we are born free, so should we or should we not exercise that freedom of thought, without fear, without restraint, and think freely before we act...

4 HOW THINGS HAPPEN?

For any incident to occur there are five basic things necessary.
1. Source of energy.
2. Conversion of energy into work and the time required for the same.
3. The means to convert energy into work.
4. Space to do the work.
5. Availability of all the above parameters at the same time and at the same place.

To understand the above facts let us take an example of working of a factory.

The essential factors would be
(i)   Source of energy - Electricity and workers.
(ii) Conversion of energy to work- the worker must do the assigned work.
(iii) Means to convert energy to work- machines, raw material, tools etc.
(iv) Space- to house machines, workers, raw material etc.
(v)   Availability of all the above parameters at the same time. If electricity is available only in the first shift, worker only in the second shift and raw material only in the third shift, nothing would happen. Many a time, such simultaneous availability is attributed to fate and in turn attributed to God- a convenient shelter when logic fails. This is not the reality.

Let us take a simple example. You want to draw and paint a picture of sunrise in water colour. The necessary things are-
1. Source of energy- You should be physically and mentally prepared to draw the painting.
2. Means- Drawing board, drawing paper, water colour box, pencil, eraser, brushes, water and water bowl etc.
3. Conversion of energy- into the act of drawing and painting and time required for the same.
4. Space- A well illuminated calm place to enable you to draw.

5.   Fate- Availability of all the above things simultaneously.

If you are not willing or physically and / or mentally unprepared, the act of painting would not start at all for want of the source of energy.

If you do not have the drawing paper or if you do not have the required water colours the painting cannot take place for want of equipment or means.

If you are available but do not work or do not take efforts to paint, no painting would proceed for want of ability to convert energy into work. If you have no time still you cannot convert the energy into work.

If your house is full of guests, you cannot draw for want of space. If you are drawing in the evening or at night with no electricity you cannot draw for want of a properly lit space as required.

If all of the above things are not available at the same time and at the same place e.g. If you are in Delhi and your equipments are in Mumbai, even if all the first four conditions are met nothing would happen.

If you start painting the lights go off! When power is restored you get guests. After the guests go, you feel sleepy. That is fate.

Whatever we have seen so far are the external factors that lead to occurrence of an incident. In addition there are internal factors viz. working of mind of an individual or the minds of a group of people directed towards a specific end.

Though there may appear a little mix-up in chronological order or simultaneous working of one or more steps in the mind, for the purpose of analysis and understanding the following steps explained with the context of drawing a painting will suffice.

1. IMAGINATION OR DEVELOPMENT OF AN IDEA-

First your mind must develop a picture of sunrise. However hazy or broad the picture may be, the visualization of sunrise is the first step. As you proceed with drawing or the painting activity it may develop further. It is an outlet for creative and constructive capacity of your mind. Your originality, individuality, inherent abilities manifest into the paintings. It is an expression of your thoughts and emotions.

2. ASPIRATION/AMBITION/WILL POWER/MOTIVATION/DESIRE-

Whatever you may call it there should be an urge in your mind, sometimes may be with a little reluctance, to start your "engine". Will power can lead to extraordinary creations from apparently ordinary persons. A typical example is if you keep a 5 meter long, 30 centimeter wide plank at the height of 30 centimeter from the ground, any one could walk over it but if it is kept at a 30 meter height very few whose will power or desire do not conflict with their imagination (that they may fall down and die) would walk across!

3. PLANNING-

Once you imagine and desire to draw, a number of queries are raised and answered in your mind. What to draw? Where to draw? When to draw? How to draw? You determine a systematic process plan of sequential activities that are to be followed and the same is continuously monitored and modified till the act is over.

4. APPLICATION OF YOUR MIND AND BODY - FOR THE WORK-

When you apply your mind, your imagination, emotions, thoughts, feed back through your sight, make your hands work fast in coordination. The mind continuously gives directives. Application of the mind and body is thinking and hard work. Nothing worthwhile can ever be achieved without deep thinking and hard work.

5. CONCENTRATION-

Better the concentration better the coordination between your hands, eyes, thought, imagination and emotions. Your mind will not get diverted anywhere else. Better the concentration better the painting.

6. ALERTNESS-

All throughout the painting process, you must be alert not to spoil your own idea, not to erase unnecessarily, not to use the wrong colour, not to spill water and so on. Otherwise all efforts may go futile.

7. DISCIPLINE-

Nothing can be achieved without discipline. Discipline in this context does not mean abiding by some laws or rules and regulations but it is a self discipline of neatness and cleanliness. It won't take a fraction of a second to spoil the entire painting if you keep colours any where, sharpen the pencil and throw the husk any where, keep the water any where and so on.

8. DEDICATION-

Applying your brain and brawn is dedication. If you do not dedicate yourself to the act of painting it may get completed but would lack the quality or excellence and moreover would not satisfy you. Dedication results in perfect coordination of your desires, aspirations, imagination, motivation, discipline and concentration which ultimately leads to satisfaction and contentment.

9. DEVOTION-

Devotion is putting up your 'heart' in the job. If you do not devote yourself, your emotions would not reflect in your job. Devotion would put 'life' into your painting.

10. DETERMINATION-

Determination is firmness of your mind. Your desires and imagination would continuously fight. "Can you draw a good painting?" "Forget, it is not within your capacity". "You have wasted enough of time, paper and colour; It is enough!" If the initiative given by your aspiration and imagination is not supplemented by 'finishiative' through your determination your painting will never be complete!

11. EFFORTS-

All the above 'ten' points form the part of the efforts that convert 'energy' into 'work'. Without efforts nothing happens. 'FACTA NON VERBA'. Just by praying, vowing or seeking blessings and without any serious efforts will not result in any outcome.

Oh! Every time so many things happen in the mind. How much time do such thing take? They take just a fraction of a second! You get down at a railway station, you see a blind handicapped fellow, finish all the above 11 activities in a fraction of a second, give him a coin and walk off! All the external and internal factors leading to the occurrence of an incident should be carefully studied and understood. Once you understand this mechanism you will know the futility of vowing in front of deities, surrendering to and sacrificing living beings in front of deities etc.

Giving offerings to non existing deities, to confess and ask for punishment in front of virtual God, bow and sit with folded hands in front of opportunistic, selfish and greedy people projecting themselves as saints with the help of some miracles is no way to achieve something or make things happen as per your expectations.

As you have seen, fate is the simultaneous availability of various external factors that lead to occurrence of an incident. The other way to look at it is fate represents factors beyond your control. There is no point in blaming one's fate. The physical, financial and cultural heritage one gets from one's parents, the country, the society, the culture and development of that society, the knowledge of the mankind during the era when you were born are all influential factors which determine and affect your fate and you have no control over it.

Man is architect of his own fortune. From dependence on rains and rivers he developed the art of digging wells and building dams and canals to get water supply. You have to make things happen. If frequent failure of electric supply is the problem, do not blame on fate. If it is home or shop use emergency lamp or inverter. If it is factory use generator and overcome the problem.

The other factors within the control of human beings are creation of good will though good words, good deeds, service and benefaction.

THE DAFFODIL PRINCIPLE

Several times my daughter had telephoned to say, "Mother, you must come see the daffodils before they are over." I wanted to go, but it was a two-hour drive from Laguna to Lake Arrowhead. "I'll come next Tuesday," I promised (a little reluctantly) on her third call.

Next Tuesday dawned cold and rainy. Still... I had promised, and so I drove. When finally I walked into Carolyn's house and hugged and greeted my grandchildren, I said,

"Forget the daffodils, Carolyn! The road is invisible in the clouds and fog and there's nothing in the world except you and these children that I want to see bad enough to drive another inch!"

My daughter smiled calmly and said, "We drive in this all the time, Mother." "Well, you won't get me back on the road until it clears and then I'm heading for home" I assured her. "I was hoping you'd take me over to the garage to pick up my car... How far is the drive?"

"Just a few blocks," Carolyn said. "I'll drive Mom. I'm used to this weather." After several minutes, I had to ask, "Where are we going? This isn't the way to the car garage!"

"We're going to my garage the long way," Carolyn grinned, "by way of the daffodils." "Carolyn," I said sternly, "please turn around."

"It's all right, Mother, I promise. You'll never forgive yourself if you miss this experience."

After twenty minutes, we turned onto a narrow gravel road and I saw a small house. On the far side of the house, I saw a hand lettered sign that read, "DAFFODIL GARDEN." We got out of the car and each took a child's hand. I followed Carolyn down the path. Then we turned a corner and I looked up and gasped.

Right before me lay the most glorious sight! It looked as though someone had taken a great vat of gold and poured it down over the mountain peak and slopes. The flowers were planted in majestic swirling patterns, great ribbons and swaths of deep orange... white... lemon yellow... salmon pink... saffron... and butter yellow.

Each different colored variety was planted as a group so that it swirled and flowed like its own river with its own unique hue. Altogether, there were five acres of daffodils.

"But who has done this?" I asked Carolyn. "It's just one woman," Carolyn answered. "She lives on the property and that's home." Carolyn pointed to a well kept A-frame house that looked small and modest in the midst of all that glory. We walked up to the house.

On the patio we saw a large poster. It read, "Answers to the Questions I Know You Are Asking." The first answer was a simple one. "50,000 bulbs," it read. The second answer was, "One at a time, by one woman. Two hands, two feet, and very little brain." The third answer was "Began in 1958."

For me that moment was a life changing experience. I thought about this woman who I had never met. More than forty years ago she had begun (one bulb at a time) to bring her vision of beauty and joy to an obscure mountaintop.

This unknown woman had forever changed the world in which she lived. She had created something of indescribable magnificence, beauty and inspiration.

The principle her Daffodil Garden taught is one of the greatest principles of celebration. That is: learning to move toward our goals and desires one step at a time-- often just one baby step at a time-- and learning to love the doing. When we multiply tiny pieces of time with small increments of daily effort, we too till find we can accomplish magnificent things... We can change the world!

"It makes me sad in a way," I admitted to Carolyn. "What might I have accomplished if I had thought of a wonderful goal thirty-five or forty years ago and had worked away at it 'one bulb at a time' through all those years. Just think what I might have been able to achieve."

My daughter summed up the message of the day in her usual direct way. "Start tomorrow," she said.

It's so pointless to think of the lost hours of yesterday. The most desirable way to make learning 'a lesson of celebration' ...instead of a cause for regret... is simply to ask, "How can I put this to use today?"

Epilogue :-

i) Every day well lived brings happy memories of the past and a vision of hope for tomorrow.

ii) No one can go back and make a brand new start. Anyone can start from now and make a brand new ending.

iii) The reward of a thing well done is to have done it.

5 HAPPINESS

When what you think, what you say and what you do are in harmony, you feel happy.

Everyone hates sorrow. Everyone seeks happiness. Everyone strives to reduce or avoid sadness.

When you are extremely thirsty, you drink cold water. You feel happy when your thirst gets quenched. When you are hungry, you eat food, you feel satisfied. Tastier the food more is your happiness. You listen to good music, you see a panoramic view, you feel happy.

One therefore, feels that satisfying your needs and satisfying the need of your senses is happiness. All happiness arising out of satisfying our senses is momentary, e.g. If you like cake and you are only given cake for breakfast, lunch, snacks and dinner, then the next day you would not only hate to eat it but also would hate to see a cake!

Real happiness is one which is not arising out of satisfying the five senses, but arising out of mental satisfaction. Gratification is not happiness.

'Sad' and 'glad' are two basic emotions. (Fear, anger, compassion, forgiveness, vengefulness are other emotions) Lack of happiness does not mean sadness and lack of sadness does not mean happiness.

When a person is disgusted, disheartened or disturbed he is unhappy. When a person is not satisfied or contented, he is unhappy.

Should one be dissatisfied? Unless a person is dissatisfied he would not have aspirations and ambitions. Without ambitions there would be no progress and development. Then will happiness and progress not go together?

Let us consider a student appearing for an important examination. If he aspires to stand first in the examination, he would be happy striving for it and working for his goal. But if after the

examination he stands second instead of first, then-
  (i)   He would be unhappy and blame the examiners and the institution conducting the examination, or
 (ii) He would blame himself, or
(iii) He would appreciate the intellect and efforts of the student ranking first, be happy for being ahead of others and make more efforts to get the top rank, or
(iv) He would be disheartened, disgusted, disappointed and leave the studies or may even turn to gambling and addiction.

When his conscience helps him and he has restrained himself he would follow the path (iii) above. In short, with conscience, balanced mind and restraint one has to reach a compromise between ambition and satisfaction to get happiness.

$$Happiness = \frac{1}{Expectations}$$

This is the master equation of happiness. Infinite expectations give zero happiness and zero expectations yield infinite happiness.

To be happy you have to give up blame, cribbing, complaining, criticising and giving excuses. Give up the need to meet expectations of others and to impress others. Give up your insistence to control all the things and be always right. Give up attachments and fear.

Does any person consider the availability of food, clothing, housing, health, education and entertainment that he enjoys today and compare with those that were available ten or hundred or thousand years ago to the mankind and consider himself happy? No!

Desires are unending like waves of sea, before one dies down, another arises. There is no end to desires.

Why does one feel sad? There are four basic reasons which cause sadness. 1. Fear 2. Greed 3. Hatred, Jealousy, enmity, envy etc. and 4. Worry.

1. FEAR-

Fear is the main reason of sadness. Why does one have fear?

(a) Fear of death- Desire to live is the basic logic of the mind. Fear of death exists not only in human beings but in all living things.

Unless one develops self confidence that no one can reduce his life even by a fraction of a second, this fear is difficult to get rid of. Highly moral and helpful behaviour brings that confidence.

(b) Fear of loss of reputation- Those who indulge in criminal activities like theft, robbery, killings, fraud, adultery, adulteration, cheating, extortion, terrorism etc. always possess the fear of getting caught by the law, face disgrace and humiliation. Persons with high morality have no such fears.

(c) Fear of oppression, humiliation, exploitation, terrorism etc.- This fear exists even in persons with high moral and benevolent attitude as this depends on morality of society and law and order situation existing in the surroundings. If the crime rate is high in society, corruption is rampant forbidding proper protection of law abiding citizens, then this fear grows. The rulers of the country and pressure of humanity on these rulers can only improve the situation.

(d) Enmity- Many reasons lead to enmity. Enmity creates continuous fear that enemy may harass, torture, humiliate, insult you and so on.

(e) Fear of Failure- Whenever you are appearing for an interview or examination or doing some work, the fear of failure results in depression, disgust, despair.

2. GREED-

Desires of mind for money, prestige and power and desires of senses create continuously growing demands which never get satisfied and this dissatisfaction creates sorrow.

3. HATRED / JEALOUSY / ENVY / ABHORRENCE-

Ego creates a feeling that others should not get what you have. Your power, possessions, authority, skills, knowledge, success, popularity etc. should be better than others. These feelings continuously haunt your mind generating hatred, jealousy, envy and abhorrence. All these lead to suspicion, distrust, disharmony, lack of peace and sadness.

4. WORRY-

Some people develop a habit of worrying. Anywhere they go

even trifles worry them. They start imagining calamities befalling them. Their anxiety leads to loss of appetite, loss of sleep, increase in blood pressure, increase in acidity, mental tension and many problems. Only engaging your mind and body continuously in work can keep away your worries.

To get rid of unhappiness, dissatisfaction, you must forget the good things you have done for others and bad things that others have done to you.

If we were to summarize, what do we conclude? Enthusiasm, contentment and discipline add pleasure to your work if it is without expectations. Be happy, be contented, be satisfied with what you have. Never leave your attempts to improve the situation. Your aspirations and ambitions should have a realistic co-relation with the existing situation.

Anything done with selfish motives invariably leads to sorrow and anything done selflessly for the wellbeing of others leads to happiness.

Those who share grief of others, themselves develop tremendous power to face calamities and their own grief. Those who follow moral practices keeping themselves away from crime, terrorism, corruption, oppression, exploitation etc. are always happy.

Live simply. Give more, expect less. Be happy. Make it a rule of life, never to regret and never to look back. Regret is an apalling waste of energy. You can not built on it.

Only human beings can smile and laugh. It is an indication of joy, happiness and pleasure. To show your affection, acquaintance, gratitude, good wishes you smile. Sarcastic laugh, fraudulent laugh, horrid laughs should be avoided.

Let us be happy and make others happy.

BE HAPPY BY MAKING OTHERS HAPPY

Two men, both seriously ill, occupied the same hospital room. One man was allowed to sit up in his bed for an hour each afternoon to help drain the fluid from his lungs. His bed was next to the room's only window. The other man had to spend all his time flat on his back. The men talked for hours on end. They spoke of their wives and families, their homes, their jobs, their involvement in the military service, where they had been on vacation..

Every afternoon, when the man in the bed by the window could sit up, he would pass the time by describing to his roommate all the things he could see outside the window. The man in the other bed began to live for those one hour periods where his world would be broadened and enlivened by all the activity and colour of the world outside.

The window overlooked a park with a lovely lake. Ducks and swans played on the water while children sailed their model boats. Young lovers walked arm in arm amidst flowers of every colour and a fine view of the city skyline could be seen in the distance.

As the man by the window described all this in exquisite details, the man on the other side of the room would close his eyes and imagine this picturesque scene.

One warm afternoon, the man by the window described a parade passing by. Although the other man could not hear the band - he could see it in his mind's eye as the gentleman by the window portrayed it with descriptive words. Days, weeks and months passed.

One morning, the day nurse arrived to bring water for their baths only to find the lifeless body of the man by the window, who had died peacefully in his sleep. She was saddened and called the hospital attendants to take the body away.

As soon as it seemed appropriate, the other man asked if he could be moved next to the window. The nurse was happy to make the switch, and after making sure he was comfortable, she left him alone.

Slowly, painfully, he propped himself up on one elbow to take his first look at the real world outside. He strained to slowly turn to look out from the window besides the bed. It faced a blank wall.

The man asked the nurse what could have compelled his deceased roommate who had described such wonderful things outside this window. The nurse responded that the man was blind and could not even see the wall.

She said, 'Perhaps he just wanted to encourage you.'
Epilogue:

There is tremendous happiness in making others happy, despite our own situations.

Shared grief is half the sorrow, but happiness when shared, is doubled.

If you want to feel rich, just count all the things you have that money can't buy.

6 TRUTH

Truth always prevails! One should always be truthful in his dealings. A person speaking the truth does not have to strain himself to remember what he said. Truth can survive the test of time. One never has to repent when he sides with the truth.

The discretionary power of intelligence which enables it to discern between truth and untruth is conscience. Your behaviour, thoughts and emotions should always be controlled by your conscience. Conscience gives you a stable, balanced and firm mind.

While being truthful one has to remember that there are certain exception which guide whether you should speak the truth or not under certain specific conditions and circumstances.

In the following exceptional cases, it is acceptable, pardonable and even recommended to avoid speaking the truth.

   i)   If it leads to ridiculing / maligning, insulting, humiliating some one.
  ii)   If it leads to breach of secrecy.
 iii)   If it leads to treachery.
  iv)   If it becomes necessary to conceal some facts from old or ailing people or children, thieves, enemies or fools.
   v)   If it leads to killing or violence.

Also in some cases the statement may not be the truth but it is accepted as it is, with full awareness of its apparent falsehood. e.g. ''sun rises'' is known as acceptable untruth and every time one does not argue that the earth rotates and the sun does not rise or set. Similarly the things which are imperative or taken for granted need not necessarily be highlighted.

In short, considering the place, time, period and the motive and its effect on an individual, society and mankind, one can judge with his own conscience what is ''truth'' and what is ''untruth''; what should be revealed and what should be concealed.

How to know the truth?

1)   By knowledge from 5 senses
2)   By knowledge from equipment that enhance the capacity of 5 senses
(loudspeakers, microscopes, telescopes, binoculars, ultrasonic equipment)
3)   By logic- cause-effect analysis, analogy, extrapolation, interpolation.
4)   By comparison
5)   By examples
6)   By tracing origin
7)   By removal of doubts
8)   By non existence or lack (Lack of heat is cold, lack of light is darkness.)
9)   By inference from experiments and observations.
Even if, you are a minority of one, truth is truth. Truth stands even without public support.

Purity is another form of truth. Adulteration of food and drugs is distortion of truth and purity and is detrimental to the society and mankind. Adulteration of food and drugs should be considered one of the greatest crimes next only to killings.

Deliberate contamination of water is another distortion of purity and deserves equal condemnation. It is detrimental to the life of human beings, animals and the plant kingdom.

Pollution of air threatening purity of air and affecting the life of human beings is one of the greatest threats at present. The entire mankind should unite to fight this at a global level. Petrol and diesel engines, coal based thermal power stations, fluorocarbons, chemical and allied industries mainly contribute towards air pollution. Increased greenery and plantation and simultaneous efforts to reduce air pollution through science and technology as well as through legislation and its effective implementation is essential.

Another threat to purity is noise pollution which may turn the next generation partially deaf. Music should discern between sweet melody and harsh sound.

Many persons tend to believe that whatever is postulated by

some "holy" persons is only the truth. They believe that a particular tradition, a particular custom, a particular practice, certain scriptures, saying of certain persons must be accepted and followed even though they are not beneficial to the society. This falsehood of thought, beliefs, understandings and concepts must be defeated by conscience and intellectual reasoning. If certain traditions and practices were useful and advisable during a particular time frame, under certain social conditions, at a specific place, they may not stand the test of time and universality. We should sense their time limit and outdatedness and show courage to reject them. A society chained by useless and outdated traditions can never progress. If we are convinced that a practice or tradition is detrimental to the society, we must have the courage to reject it even though it may be supported by the so called holy persons or holy books.

Hypocrisy, deceit and ostentation are untruthfulness. Pretend and talk of trust in nonviolence, love, compassion, justice and friendship and actually practice crookedness, wickedness, injustice and violence.

Let us avoid ostentation and hypocrisy. Let us be truthful to ourselves, society and mankind.

The 8 universal truths are as follows :-

 1. There is no heaven up above or anywhere.

 2. There is no hell down below or anywhere.

 3. There are no ghosts.

 4. There never was and never will be a day of judgement.

 5. There are no miracles sleight of hand and illusions are claimed as miracles.

 6. There is no GOD.

 7. There is no soul.

 8. There is no rebirth.

Chicken

A Woman walks into a butchery shop just before closing time and asks,

"Do you still have chicken?"

The butcher opens his deep freezer, takes out his only chicken left and puts it on the weighing scale. It weighs 1.5 kg.

The woman looks at the chicken and at the scale and asked,
"Do you have one that's a bit bigger than this one ?"

The butcher puts his only chicken back into the freezer, and then takes it out again.

But this time when he puts it on the scale, he craftily keeps his thumb on the scale pan.

And the scale now shows 2 kg.

"That's wonderful," said the woman.

"I'll take both of them, please!"

In a situation like this, you realize at once that your integrity and reputation are firmly on the line.

Your wisdom becomes foolishness, and your cunningness becomes stupidity.

Until now the butcher has his head inside the big deep freezer, looking for the first chicken.
Remember:

1. Always tell the truth, and you will be free !!! Truth by nature is self evident.

2. A good name is better than riches.

3. Live to express yourself, and not to impress others.

7 NON KILLING / NON VIOLENCE

We differentiate the entire world into two broad categories, those who have life are living things and those who do not have life are non-living. To totally avoid killing is non killing, often referred to as total non violence.

Desire to live is the basic logic of all living things and to live is their basic right. To deprive this fundamental right to live is the greatest crime from religious, moral, legal or any point of view. Non-killing should be the supreme principle of humanity.

All carnivorous animals live by getting their food by killing other animals. Even human beings largely depend on sheep, goat, chicken, duck, fish etc. for their food. All vegetarians depend on plant kingdom for their food. Plants are also living things. Then can we conclude that the entire mankind survives only by depriving life from some animals or plant? Does it mean that non-violence is a theoretical concept and can not be put into practice?

Nonviolence is a perfectly practical concept. It is not only preached but practised from the era of Mahavir and Gautam Buddha and in 20th century-canvassed and practised by Mahatma Gandhi. In order that a common person living in any part of the world can practice nonviolence, the following guidelines will be useful.

(1) A human being should avoid killing a human being. By inventing medicines for incurable diseases, the threat to the human life should be reduced. Small pox, plague, tuberculosis are on the verge of getting totally eradicated, cholera, typhoid, malaria etc. are under control. Desperate search for medicines on AIDS is going on the world over. There is substantial progress to cure cancer.

(2) Even though germs are living things, killing of the germs and insects hazardous to mankind and plants can not be treated as violence.

(3) Unknowingly killing microscopic, sub microscopic and exceedingly small living beings should not be treated as killing.

(4) Killing of animals, fish and plants for basic need of food,

shelter, clothing, medicine and education seems to be unavoidable. To cultivate and breed these plants and animals at least to the extent they are consumed becomes the responsibility of mankind e.g. Those who consume eggs and chicken should directly or indirectly contribute to development of poultry.

One should try to resort to vegetarian food and avoid killing of animals for food. Those who are dependent on non-vegetarian food should observe at least one day a week as a meatless day and slowly try to achieve 100% vegetarianism wherever feasible.

Conscience of humanity needs to be awakened in regard to the cruelties inflicted on dumb, defenceless creatures that are being slain the world over to feed human beings. Hands are to be used to bless and not to slaughter. Hands are to be used to help and heal and not to harm.

(5) Killing as a part of duty which does not have any selfish motive like revenge, abhorrence, anger, hatred, greed, temptation, passion etc. is pardonable e.g. killings by armed forces or police service personnel.

(6) Killings to protect life of yourself, your father/mother/ brother/sister/children/friends etc. as a moral or social duty without any personal motive is pardonable.

(7) Accidental death because of reasons beyond your control, without any motive or intention to kill, if not caused by carelessness or unsafe practices may be pardonable.

Normally motive behind the killing will dictate if the act is pardonable or not. Otherwise the effects of the act on individuals, society and the entire mankind may help to identify, if it is pardonable or not.

(8) Is it fair to execute criminals? Should capital punishment be abolished? In this civilised world is hanging not a barbarous act? Few countries have abolished capital punishment. But the capital punishment does not have a limited intention of "life for life" or "a tooth for a tooth" principle. It is in fact a warning to several other budding criminals that their life will not be spared if they resort to crime.

One must bear in mind that whenever you kill someone he is

a son or daughter of someone, brother or sister of someone, father or mother of someone, husband or wife of someone or a friend of someone. One must think before killing someone as to what he or she would feel if his or her near and dear one is killed or if he is killed what impact it will have on his relatives and friends. If one thinks on these lines, he would never kill.

If your thoughts can control your emotions, killing will stop. Do not suppress your emotion but wait till emotions die down and thoughts take over.

Violence is a broad term, which not only covers killing but involves damage to the mind, body and property.

Unfortunately human beings have not come to a stage to get rid of wars and fights. Mutual distrust, suspicion, and lack of understanding lead to war. Crime in society is the main cause of violence. Theft, adultery, atrocities, corruption, exploitation, oppression, suppression, terrorism, gambling and addiction are ten main spokes of the wheel of crime.

In case of incurable disease, unbearable pain, impending death, patient in coma, euthanasia is acceptable, however, proper legal precaution need to be taken to ensure that it is not misused.

STARFISH

A man was walking down the beach at sunset. As he walked along, he saw another man in the distance. He noticed this man kept leaning down, picking up something and throwing it out into the water, again and again. As, he approached even closer, he noticed that the man was picking up starfish that had been washed up on the beach.

He was throwing them back into the water, one by one.

Puzzled, he approached the man and said,

"Good Evening. I was wondering what you are doing."

"I'm throwing these starfish back into the ocean. You see, it's low tide and all these starfish have been washed up onto the shore. If I don't throw them back into the ocean, they'll die up here from lack of oxygen."

"But, there must be thousands of starfish on this beach. You can't possibly get to all of them. And, don't you realize this is probably happening on hundreds of beaches all up and down this coast. Can't you see that you can't possibly make a difference?"

The man bent down and picked up yet another starfish, and threw it back into the ocean. With a smile he replied, "Made a difference to that one!!!"

Just remember, no matter how small the deed, it really does make a difference.

Make a difference today. Do something for someone, even a tiny deed filled with love, will make you a Star in the ocean.

Use your hands to save life not to take life.

8 LOVE

Of all qualifications, love is the most important, for if you get it you need nothing else and without it all the rest acquisitions are meaningless. Constant happiness can only be achieved through love and compassion associated with wisdom.

Wherever human relations exist, love exists. Between father and child, mother and child, brothers and sisters, friends, neighbors, colleagues, teacher and pupil, boss and subordinate, husband and wife, infinite relations.

The power and influence of love is much more than the threat of the worst punishment, torture or even fear of death.

Love is the ultimate art of giving. Real love does not expect anything in return.

Love kills jealousy, envy, hatred and abhorrence. Love kills enmity and vengeance.

Love is an emotion. You love your kiths and kins. You love your pets. You love your home, your school, your village, your country. Thus love is not only restricted to human beings but it extends to other animals and non-living things as well. Let us develop love as a virtue which will help us to love all human beings, animal-kingdom and plant-kingdom.

Love and equality go hand in hand. Love does not differentiate between the poor and the rich, black and white, man or woman, old or young, negro or mongol, your countryman or foreigner.

Hypocritical love conceals motives of lust, passion, greed and temptation. Real love is associated with spontaneity, honesty, integrity, respect and sacrifice. Not only human beings but even animals are known to sacrifice their lives for their love!

Love gives you happiness. Love gives you contentment. Love gives you peace.

Good will, well wishes, congratulations and blessings express affection and love.

Bestow upon the world love without expecting even a mention

of gratitude in return.

Tears from the affectionate will publish the love within.

The loveless belong to themselves alone, the loving people belong to others till their bones.

Love not only sustains virtue but it restrains evil as well.

Every thought you think changes your biochemistry. Your hormones are affected by your thoughts. Pay attention to stuff that bring you joy. Look for things that bring you a smile!

INSTALLING LOVE

Customer : Well, I'm not very technical, but I think I'm ready to install it now. What do I do first?

Tech Support : The first step is to open your HEART. Have you located your HEART, ma'am?

Customer : Yes, I have, but there are several other programs running right now. Is it okay to install while they are running?

Tech Support : What programs are running, ma'am?

Customer : Let's see... I have PAST-HURT.EXE, LOW-ESTEEM.EXE, GRUDGE. EXE, and RESENTMENT.COM running now.

Tech Support : No problem. Love will gradually erase PAST-HURT.EXE from your current operating system. It may remain in your permanent memory, but it will no longer disrupt other programs. LOVE will eventually overwrite LOW-ESTEEM.EXE with a module of its own called HIGH-ESTEEM.EXE. However, you have to completely turn off GRUDGE.EXE and RESENTMENT.COM. Those programs prevent LOVE from being properly installed. Can you turn those off, ma'am?

Customer : I don't know how to turn them off. Can you tell me how?

Tech Support : My pleasure. Go to your Start menu and invoke FORGIVENESS. EXE. Do this as many times as necessary until it's erased the programs you don't want.

Customer : Okay, now LOVE has started installing itself automatically. Is that normal?

Tech Support : Yes. You should receive a message that says it will reinstall for the life of your HEART. Do you see that message?

Customer : Yes, I do. Is it completely installed?

Tech Support : Yes, but remember that you have only the base program. You need to begin connecting to other HEARTs in order to get the upgrades.

Customer : Got it. Hey! My HEART is filling up with new files. SMILE.MPG is playing on my monitor right now and it shows that PEACE.EXE, and CONTENTMENT. COM are copying themselves all over my HEART. Is this normal?

Tech Support : Sometimes. For others it takes a while, but eventually everything gets downloaded at the proper time. So, LOVE is installed and running. You should be able to handle it from here. Ah, one more thing.

Customer : Yes?

Tech Support : LOVE is freeware. Be sure to give it and its various modules to everybody you meet. They will in turn share it with other people and they will return some similarly cool modules back to you.

Customer : I will! Thanks for your help!

9 LIBERTY

Liberty is absence of coercion. Liberty is the birth right of all human beings. Liberty is the right which should be enjoyed without forgetting one's duty of non encroaching on the liberty of others.

Not to have a benevolent and co-operative attitude towards others and not to have an understanding and consideration for others is a vice. Empathy should go hand in hand with liberty, otherwise it would get converted into reckless freedom and ultimately lead to chaos.

As a part of freedom all children below 18 years of age have the following rights-
1. Right to play,
2. Right to education,
3. Right to obtain food, clothes, shelter and safety from parents/ guardians/society,
4. Right not to work to earn living. Employing and exploiting children for work should be strictly punishable.

The rights of a free adult are-
1. Right for freedom of speech and writing,
2. Right to select one's own profession/trade/business,
3. Right to select one's own religion,
4. Right to acquire property,
5. Right to protect his/her kin's life and property.
6. Right to choose his government.

Social freedom will always accompany equality, fraternity and justice.

If this civilization is to survive and thrive, liberty and liberals should win over superstitious, hedonists and fanatics.

Slavery, bonded labour, exploitation are enemies of liberty.

If a human being is looked at as a "useful commodity" then how to utilise it to maximise its utility value gets considered. This leads to exploitation and oppression. This leads to slavery. One forgets whether the person is your mother or daughter, father or son, brother or sister, friend or neighbour, colleague or subordinate. Never look at any human being as a commodity. Treat every human being as a human being with dignity and respect. Freedom is not worth having, if it does not connote freedom to err.

Freedom is never dear at any price. It is breath of life.

Freedom of expression through writing, speech, drawings, cartoons, animation is basic. Decency, decorum and dignity should be maintained while enjoying freedom of expression. No abusive language, no intimidation, no threatening, no encroachment on privacy , no violence, no destruction of property and life.

It would be dictatorial and authoritative to outlaw and criminalise the resentments, criticism and insults that curb the freedom of expression. Gagging any voice of dissent by arresting people under the name of law and order is uncalled for unless it is violence causing destruction of property and life. Individual and society must develop immunity to take offensive and insulting comments. The message carried by criticism should be taken without offending the messenger.

Can I Borrow Rs...50?

A woman came home from work late, tired and irritated, to find her 5-year old son waiting for her at the door.

SON: 'Mummy, may I ask you a question?'

MUM: 'Yeah sure, what it is?' replied the woman.

SON: 'Mummy, how much do you make an hour?'

MUM: 'That's none of your business. Why do you ask such a thing?' the woman said angrily.

SON: 'I just want to know. Please tell me, how much do you make an hour?'

MUM: 'If you must know, I make Rs.150 an hour.'

SON: 'Oh,' the little boy replied, with his head down.

SON: 'Mummy, may I please borrow Rs.50?'

The mother was furious, 'If the only reason you asked that is so you can borrow some money to buy a silly toy or some other nonsense, then you march yourself straight to your room and go to bed. Think about why you are being so selfish. I don't work hard everyday for such childish frivolities.' The little boy quietly went to his room and shut the door.. The woman sat down and started to get even angrier about the little boy's questions. How dare he asks such questions only to get some money? After about an hour or so, the woman had calmed down , and started to think:

Maybe there was something he really needed to buy with that Rs.50 and he really didn't ask for money very often.The woman went to the door of the little boy's room and opened the door. 'Are you asleep, son?' She asked. 'No Mummy, I'm awake,' replied the boy. 'I've been thinking, maybe I was too hard on you earlier' said the woman. 'It's been a long day and I took out my aggravation on you. Here's the Rs.50 you asked for.' The little boy sat straight up, smiling. 'Oh, thank you Mummy!' he yelled. Then, reaching under his pillow he pulled out some crumpled up bills. The woman saw that the boy already had money, started to get angry again.

The little boy slowly counted out his money, and then looked up at his mother. 'Why do you want more money if you already have some?' the mother grumbled. Because I didn't have enough, but now I do,' the little boy replied. 'Mummy, I have Rs.150 now. Can I buy an hour of your time? Please come home early tomorrow. I would like to have dinner with you.' The mother was crushed.. She put his arms around her little son, and she begged for his forgiveness.

It's just a short reminder to all of you working so hard in life. We should not let time slip through our fingers without having spent some time with those who really matter to us, those close to our hearts. Do remember to share that Rs.150 worth of your time with someone you love.. If we die tomorrow, the company that we are working for could easily replace us in a matter of hours. But the family and friends we leave behind will feel the loss for the rest of their lives.

10 EQUALITY

"Worst part of equality is to make unequal things equal." Aristotle The world equality is often misunderstood. The sarcastic saying, "All are equal but some are more equal" is outcome of this misunderstanding.

Distinctness, diversity are natural but to divide humanity on this basis as superior and inferior, upper class and lower class is unfair, unjust and incorrect.

Equality should be established by eliminating discrimination on the basis of race, religion, gender, colour, caste, creed, country, ethnic origin etc. Inequality or discrimination on the basis of knowledge, competence, expertise, skill, intelligence, ability, dexterity and performance is unavoidable, but each and every human being should get a fair or equal opportunity to acquire skills or knowledge.

Caste, illiteracy, discrimination against woman, exploitation of labour, oppression of poor, ostracisation from society, untouchability are enemies of equality.

Equality does not mean that the President of a country and his peon should have equal salaries and facilities. But if capable and competent the peon should have an opportunity and freedom even to become the President.

In any educational field, trade, profession, service or sports no one should be denied entry because of his race, religion, caste, creed, gender, tradition/ custom or family background e.g. If the required competence in physics, chemistry and mathematics is there, a person should not be denied engineering education.

Carpenters, black smiths, plumbers, masons, electricians, mechanics should not be denied equal status with doctors, engineers, advocates, politicians etc. Dignity of labour and recognition of excellence is the basic foundation of equality.

To discriminate between man and woman as one is superior to the other only on the basis of gender is unfair, incorrect and detrimental to mankind. In any society men and women should have equal opportunities, respect, status and right. Physical differences should be harnessed to play supplementary and complimentary rolls to each other. Every man or woman can contribute to the welfare and well being of the society to the best of his/her abilities. Attributing secondary and subsidiary role to woman by certain religions and societies has caused great loss to mankind.

It is obvious that the profession which calls for higher skills, knowledge, abilities, intelligence or involve more hard work would have better status, respect, rewards and facilities. But everyone should have fair opportunity to improve and develop one's abilities, skills, knowledge and come up.

The "vice-ego" makes one think that he/she is stronger, clever, richer, more powerful than others and breeds inequality. The possessiveness, competition and struggle to go ahead and stay ahead by surpassing others gets generated. Falsehood, ostentation, hypocrisy, sycophancy, bribing and other unfair means are often used in these unhealthy competition to go head. Pursuit never ends! Your aim may be good but your means to achieve your goal also need to be good. In your race to go ahead you cultivate inequality, and run away from reality!

One fine day you notice age is catching up, body responses are poor, circumstances change, power, position, wealth are not possessed by any one for ever. Interdependence of human beings is noticed. You notice every person is superior to every other person in at least one field. There is no one who is superior to others in every field. An apparently ordinary ward-boy in a hospital can donate blood and save life of the President of a country.

Excessive richness and excessive poverty in society is detrimental to equality. In a society nobody should be so poor that anyone can buy him and no one should be so rich that he can buy anybody. Those who "have" should not just provide to those who "have not" but should teach them how to "have" and eradicate poverty and want of minimum basic needs. To make the weak stronger, eradicate exploitation and oppression is real equality.

CRACKED POTS

A water bearer in India had two large pots, each hung on the ends of a pole which he carried across his neck. One of the pots had a crack in it, while the other pot was perfect and always delivered a full portion of water. At the end of the long walk from the stream to the house, the cracked pot arrived only half full. For a full two years this went on daily, with the bearer delivering only one and a half pots full of water to his house.

Of course, the perfect pot was proud of its accomplishments, perfect for which it was made. But the poor cracked pot was ashamed of its own imperfection, and miserable that it was able to accomplish only half of what it had been made to do.

After 2 years of what it perceived to be a bitter failure, it spoke to the water bearer one day by the stream. "I am ashamed of myself, and I want to apologize to you. I have been able to deliver only half my load because this crack in my side causes water to leak out all the way back to your house. Because of my flaws, you have to do all of this work, and you don't get full value from your efforts," the pot said.

The bearer said to the pot, "Did you notice that there were flowers only on your side of the path, but not on the other pot's side? That's because I have always known about your flaw, and I planted flower seeds on your side of the path, and every day where we walk back, you've watered them. For a year I have been able to pick these beautiful flowers to decorate the table. Without you being just the way you are, there would not be this beauty to grace the house.

Moral : Each of us has our own unique flaws. We're all cracked pots. But it's the cracks and flaws we each have that make our lives together so very interesting and rewarding. You've just got to take each person for what they are, and look for the good in them.

Blessed are the flexible, for they shall not be bent out of shape. Remember to appreciate all the different people in your life!

11 FRATERNITY

Oneness of the entire mankind on this planet earth is fraternity. The entire mankind is one family - a happy, loving family with mutual love and affection, with mutual respect and service, with willingness to sacrifice for each other. Abhorrence, jealousy, hatred, enmity, wickedness, crookedness, vengeance should vanish and harmony with mutual trust, understanding and co-operation should be established.

Fraternity crosses all limits of inequality. There is no differentiation on the basis of race, religion, cast, creed, gender or even nationality Even though every country may be different administratively, culturally, geographically and historically, all nations should unite for peaceful and co-operative coexistence. Population explosion, control of pollution of air, water and noise, environmental protection, terrorism etc. should be tackled with common interests and common aims. The physiological and security needs of food, clothing, shelter, health and education also need to be tackled together. United Nations Organization and world sports event are going to contribute significantly towards fraternity. Unity in diversity is motto of fraternity. The different languages and cultures of the world may retain their individuality but there must be a common link between them which can bring about complete understanding. A universal language, a common script and a common dress need to be adopted. English language and script should be accepted as universal language and script.

The days of building great nations and empires have come to an end. From the days of flocks, tribes, villages, towns, cities, states and nations, mankind has reached the period of the world common wealth. In an age when it was necessary to unite warring tribes and clans into a nation, love for one's country was meritorious and considered the highest from of loyalty. In the 21st century, chauvinism- extreme nationalism- would bar the way to unity of mankind into total fraternity. In the new world order, there can be no weak nations. The people on the earth would meet as equals. Their governments will each be represented in the world parliament which will be concerned with the prosperity of all nations and happiness of all mankind. The world common wealth of the future will preserve the autonomy of each nation and safeguard personal freedom. Like freedom and rights of every individual are protected in a nation the freedom and sovereignty of each nation will be protected by world parliament. The vast resources of the planet will be tapped and pooled for the benefit of all the people of the world. Uniform system of weights, measures, currency, language and script will be necessary to facilitate interaction.

Humanity united and free from the curse of war will spend enormous means and energies at its disposal towards such ends as raising standards of living, advancement of education, elimination of diseases, development of science, cultivation of arts, and elimination of crime.

If one nation dare attack another nation, the entire world should protect the attacked nation. Once this is established destruction of weapons including atomic weapons would be a reality.

Interest of the entire mankind should be kept above all interests, including national, religious and individual.

BUILDING BRIDGES

Once upon a time two brothers who lived on adjoining farms fell into conflict. It was the first serious rift in 40 years of farming side by side, sharing machinery, and trading labor and goods as needed without a hitch.

Then the long collaboration fell apart. It began with a small misunderstanding and it grew into a major difference, and finally it exploded into an exchange of bitter words followed by weeks of silence.

One morning there was a knock on the older brother's door. He opened it to find a man with a carpenter's toolbox. "I'm looking for a few days work" he said. "Perhaps you would have a few small jobs here and there. Could I help you?" "Yes," said the older brother. "I do have a job for you. Look across the creek at that farm. That's my neighbour, in fact, it's my younger brother. Last week there was a meadow between us and he took his bulldozer to the river and now there is a creek between us. Well, he may have done this to spite me, but I'll give him one better. See that pile of lumber by the barn? I want you to build me an 8 foot fence so I won't need to see his place anymore. Take this money and complete the work before I return in a weeks time.

The carpenter said, "I think I understand the situation. Show me the nails and the post-hole digger and I'll be able to do a job that pleases you."

The older brother had to go to town for supplies, so he helped the carpenter get the materials ready and then he was off for a week to other town.

The carpenter worked hard the whole week measuring, sawing, nailing. About weekend when the older brother returned, the carpenter had just finished the job. The older brother's eyes opened wide, his jaw dropped. There was no fence there at all. It was a bridge, a bridge stretching from one side of the creek to the other! A fine piece of work, handrails and all, and the neighbour, his younger brother, was coming across, his arms outstretched.

"You have build this bridge after all I've said and done." With these words they both embraced and hugged each other.

Then they turned to see the carpenter hoist his toolbox on his shoulder. "No, wait! Stay a few days. I've a lot of other projects for you," said the older brother. "I'd love to stay on," the carpenter said, "but, I have many more bridges to build."

All of us are carpenters to build bridges between each other's hearts. Love is the only material required to build. We are going to move on to build bridges of fraternity to make this earth a better place to live.

12 COMPASSION - KINDNESS

Compassion is inherent in human beings. Conditioning of the mind enhances it. Poverty, misery, sickness, scarcity, natural calamities, injustice etc. arouse emotion of compassion.

Lack of cruelty or extreme opposite to cruelty is compassion but it would be unfair to call a cruel person, a tyrant, a murderer or a robber as a person who totally lacks compassion or kindness. In fact if you observe behaviour of such person with his/her children, parents, friends, or spouse, you would notice so much of compassion that you would feel that such a person can never be cruel.

Compassion or kindness is a mixture of many virtues -love, affection, liberal attitude, gratitude, modesty, leniency, sense of responsibility, sympathy, nobleness, benefaction, fraternity, equality, forgiveness etc. Kindness eliminates many vices like enmity, revengefulness, cruelty, adamance, arrogance, jealousy, hatred etc.

Compassion is an emotion which gets generated in your mind when you sense the misery of others. You feel pity, sympathetic, regretful. You feel like offering your help-time, money, efforts- to reduce misery, to improve their condition, to enable them to surmount their problems.

When is normally your compassion aroused?

When you see a person (or persons)

1. Who is disabled- deaf, dumb, blind or lame.
2. Mentally handicapped- one who can not sense the world due to damaged brain and nervous system.
3. Suffering from an incurable disease and is in tremendous pain.
4. Caught in a natural calamity such as an earthquake, flood, cyclone, snowfall, avalanche, fire or man made calamities such as theft, robbery, accident, war, terrorism atrocities etc.
5. Who is deprived of the basic needs of food, clothes, shelters.

Compassion is not felt only for humans but for other animals as well. "Friends of animal societies" have come up every where through compassion only.

When you see an animal agonising for want of food or water, your kindness forces you to help. Seeing the misery of animals in a circus or in a zoo, your kindness is kindled.

Kindness makes you forget your ego, your selfishness, your possessiveness. It is the best medicine to control "ego- the vice" and develop a sense of love and sacrifice. To have a pet at home, helps to develop compassion.

Let us think of others and develop our virtue of compassion.

The punishment to those who have done evil is to put them to shame by showing them kindness in return and to forget both the evil and good done on both sides.

THE POWER OF A HUG

A few years ago, a set of twins were born. They were kept in separate incubators as usual, but one of them was week and not expected to live.

One of the nurses, going against hospital policy, placed both babies in the same incubator. As soon as they were reunited, the healthier twin threw her arm over her weaker sister in an endearing embrace. What happened? The little sister's temperature rose to normal and her heart rate stabilized, and she survived!

Both babies thrived and went home together. At home they continued to share a crib and were always snuggling closely. Today they are happy pre-schoolers.

Did the hospital change its policy? You bet it did! After seeing the effects of putting the two girls together, they now put siblings together. How about that! You can never underestimate the value of a hug!

Let's not forget to embrace the ones we love. May all your days be filled with hugs!

13 FORGIVENESS

Absence of revenge, retaliation, vengeance is forgiveness. Forgiveness is an attribute of strong.

Forgiveness is the ability to control anger or in the ultimate state it prevent generation of anger. Forgiveness enables one to control emotion of revenge. It controls one's desire to punish someone. Forgiveness is kindness, tenderness, affinity and love expressed and practised through emotions and thoughts.

Hypocrisy to forgive outwardly and cultivate revenge, enmity and desire to punish inwardly is not forgiveness. If one forgives under the fear that "enemy or opponents may harass me if I do not forgive" is not real forgiveness. If greed and temptation is motive behind forgiving- "If I don't forgive my motive will not be served" - then it is not real forgiveness. If your ego is dictating forgiveness- "I am powerful and I am the master and only I can forgive him and save him and in return can get my things done from him to my convenience." It is not forgiveness.

In short any forgiveness originating from ego, fear, hypocrisy, greed, lust, etc. is not real forgiveness. The selfless, motiveless, unperverted manifestation of love, kindness and affection is forgiveness- typically attributed to a mothers feelings towards her child.

"The one who ridicules me, is my benefactor as he shows my vices giving me direction to improve"- is typical forgiving attitude. "One who is depriving me of my belonging is relieving me of my greed and possessiveness and one who punishes me is giving me right atonement for my mistakes" is the attitude getting developed through forgiveness.

Without forgiveness the chain reaction of anger and revenge never breaks. 'A' troubles 'B', then 'B' takes revenge and then 'A' takes counter revenge, so the cycle of revenge and counter revenge puts both the parties in the ditch of uncertainty, fear, sorrow and anger!

If you punish your student, or daughter or son or friend or colleague with the motive to eliminate or reduce his/her vices that would result in his/her improvement or progress or development, then this punishment is not against forgiveness.

In order to ensure law, order, justice and peace in the state, if the administrators without any prejudice, lawfully punish the people, it is not against forgiveness.

In short the motive or purpose behind the forgiveness as well as its result dictates what is the correct forgiveness.

Forgiveness is an inherent virtue irrespective of who is forgiven and for what reasons he/she is forgiven. The person who is forgiven is only instrumental for the manifestation of the virtue of forgiveness and it is immaterial as to who is forgiven.

One of the most important factors about forgiveness is the ability to forget. If you learn to forget mistakes of others, anger, abhorrence, vengeance, will not get generated.

A weak mind can never forgive.

Let us follow policy of forget and forgive.

SAND AND STONE

The story goes that two friends were walking through the desert. During some point of the journey they had an argument, and one friend slapped the other one in the face.

The one who got slapped was hurt, but without saying anything, wrote in the sand: "Today my best friend slapped me in the face."

They kept on walking until they found an oasis, where they decided to take a bath. The one who had been slapped got stuck in the mire and started drowning, but the friend saved him.

After he recovered from the near drowning, he wrote on a stone: "Today my best friend saved my life."

The friend who had slapped and saved his best friend asked him, "After I hurt you, you wrote in the sand and now you write on a stone. Why?"

The other friend replied: "When someone hurts us we should write it down in sand where winds of forgiveness can erase it away. But when someone does something good for us, we must engrave it in stone where no wind can ever erase it."

LEARN TO WRITE YOUR HURTS IN THE SAND AND TO CARVE YOUR BENEFITS IN STONE.

14 PEACE

Peace is freedom from hostility and conflict. There was never a good war or a bad peace.

Peace starts from mental peace and finally develops into global peace. Global or international peace can only be achieved step by step from individual to family to society to national level to international level.

To have a peaceful mind one must get rid of lust, anger, temptation, greed, arrogance and jealousy. Once these vices are eliminated you get considerable peace. Your mental power, your courage increases, your mind is free of fear and slowly you are in a position to control the "vice-ego". Your mind will be full of love, compassion, forgiveness and freedom from fear and will lead you to total peace, through control of emotions. Meditation will help you to achieve it.

Once you achieve mental peace, anger, abhorrence, vengeance run away, greed and temptation are under control, arrogance and adamance tend to vanish. As a result, theft, deceiving, atrocities, exploitation, oppression, corruption, adulteration and terrorism continuously reduce with low crime, the social peace is established.

Social peace is impossible in a society full of deprivation and with scarcity of basic needs of food, clothes, shelter, education and health. The need for unpolluted air, contamination free water and unadulterated food is a basic must for a healthy society.

The books, magazines, television programmes are full of sex and crime. The taste of people need be changed. The way sex and crime is highlighted through media is disastrous to mankind.

The belligerent attitude of the people and countries result from lack of trust and faith in each other, suspicion, excessive nationalism and religious fanaticism. To achieve world peace and harmony in the entire mankind, the mutual understanding and co-operation should develop the atmosphere of mutual trust, faith and fraternity.

If revenge is replaced by forgiveness, compassion and benevolence, peace will result.

THE SECRET OF PEACE

An American businessman was visiting a small Spanish village when a small boat with a lone fisherman docked. Inside the boat there were a number of large fishes. He praised the quality of his fish and asked how long it took to catch them.

The Spanish replied, "Just about three hours."

The American said why didn't he stay out little longer and catch more fish, to which the Spanish replied that he had enough to support his family's immediate needs. The American then asked, "But what do you do with the rest of your time?"

The Spanish replied, "I play with my children, take siesta with my wife, spend time with my oldies, and every evening drink tequila and play guitar with my friends."

The American said, "You should spend more time fishing and with those funds buy a larger boat, and with the additional income, you could buy several boats, and eventually you will have a large fleet of fishing boats. Instead of selling to a middleman you will sell directly to the processor, eventually opening your own cannery. You will control the product, processing and distribution. You will have to leave this small village and move to New York city where you will run your expanding business."

The Spanish fisherman asked, "But how long will all this take?" To which the American said, "Perhaps 15-20 years."

"But after that?"

The American said, "Here's the best part. When the time is right you would sell your company stock to the public and become very rich, you would make millions and millions."

"Millions and millions, But after that?"

The American thought for a while, and then said, "Well, you will retire, move to a small fishing village where you will play with your children, take siesta with your wife, spend time with your oldies, and in the evenings drink tequila and play guitar with your friends."

Fisherman said, "Thanks for your advice. But then it would be too late. Childrens childhood would have been over. So neither I can enjoy playing with the children nor children can enjoy playing with father. The oldies in the house would probably be no more. If I don't spend time with wife in youth, then when would I spend time with her. Not providing time for wife may throw our marriage in flames. The friends as well as I would have become old and may have acquired increased cholesterol levels or high B. P. or diabetes or might have lost teeth and taken to denture then how can I enjoy eating and drinking with friends at that stage."

One should progress in his job, profession or business but should have proper time management to ensure that he has adequate time at right stage of life for his children, wife, old family members and friends. This is the secret of peaceful life.

15 JUSTICE

What is justice? The protection of the fundamental principles of humanitarianism is justice. To follow the laws in vogue in various countries in order to protect basic human rights for a safe and peaceful coexistence is justice.

Killing or violence deprives the basic right to live and hence amounts to the worst crime. The motive behind the killing decides the level of injustice. Killing arising out of lust, temptation, anger, desires, cruelty, vengeance deserves capital punishment. Killing while carrying out duties as a soldier, police etc. or for protection of self, family, friends and society in general in unavoidable circumstances may deserve pardon.

To follow inequality based on race, religion, caste, province, gender etc. is serious social injustice.

Terrorism, exploitation oppression, extortion, suppression are serious crimes which need severe punishment to enable law abiding, peace loving civilians to lead a calm, quite and safe life. Addiction and gambling are detrimental to individual and society from physical and financial point of view and judiciary should curb these by proper atonement.

Adulteration of food and drugs, contamination of water, endangering plant and animals along with the human being and pollution of air are serious social offenses and deserve serious punishment by law and need to be tackled with determination and firmness.

Theft, deceit, corruption, adultery are treated as punishable sins for ages but are not under control yet. Though judiciary has to play significant role in eliminating these "diseases" of society, improving morality of society and individual is the real remedy. Kidnapping children or persons for ransom money, storage, traffic and sale of narcotics are two very very serious offences which need severe punishment and eradication.

The seriousness of an unjust event has to be judged by

assessing the motives behind and its effect at individual, social and global level, immediately or in future.

Justice delayed is justice denied. To help injustice or not to resist injustice are crimes. Judiciary should fix time limit to give justice for each type of case. Written arguments in place of verbal arguments can save time.

A person who judges if a particular act is just or unjust should have a balanced mind, free from prejudices, and should not fall prey to temptation, greed or pressures.

SCATTERED PAPERS...

Once upon a time an old man spread rumors that his neighbor was a thief. As a result, the young man was arrested. Days later the young man was proven innocent. After been released he sued the old man for wrongly accusing him.

In court the old man told the judge : 'They were just comments, didn't harm anyone.'

The judge, before passing sentence on the case, told the old man : 'Write all the things you said about him on a piece of paper. Cut them up and on the way home, throw the pieces of paper out. Tomorrow, come back to hear the sentence.'

The next day, the judge told the old man : 'Before receiving the sentence, you will have to go out and gather all the pieces of paper that you threw out yesterday.'

The old man said : 'I can't do that! The wind spread them and I won't know where to find them.'

The judge then replied : ' The same way, simple comments may destroy the honour of a man to such an extent that one is not able to fix it. If you can't speak well of someone, rather don't say anything.

'Let's all be masters of our mouths, so that we won't be slaves of our words.'

16 BENEVOLENCE - GENEROSITY-MUNIFICENCE

All the above words refer to the art of giving without any expections of returns in any from. The art of giving does not involve giving the things which are of no use to you or which have no value. It does not involve giving the thing to those who do not need and cannot make proper use of what you give. True charity is to give the needy otherwise it becomes a gift of 'measured return.'

Giving your knowledge, art or skill to others is the greatest gift that you can give as the same can be utilized by the receiver for life time and in turn he/she can pass on the knowledge to others Moreover, one who 'donates' the knowledge or teaches his art and skill does not become poorer but in fact 'richer' in his knowledge. If you meet a hungry person you can give him a fish but it is still better if you teach him how to catch a fish, so that for the whole of his life he would not be hungry.

Give your love and affection to others. Let others participate in your joy. Bestow your kindness, compassion upon others. Give your thoughts, ideas, dreams, values of life to others. Give your happiness.

Give time for others. Encourage people. Appreciate them. Motivate them.

There is no generosity in offering donations to satisfy your ego that people would call you generous, rich, benevolent and so on.

If you give anything to get your work done it is corruption and not munificence.

One should give with sense of duty, with gratitude, to oblige the society, which works for you and gives you everything without expecting anything from you in return.

Blood donation is a great benevolent act.

Not only during your lifetime you can give but even after death you can donate your eyes and the entire body!

It is a must that the eligibility of a person to receive the donation should be verified. One must ensure that you donate to a proper and deserving person or institution.

Every person should donate at least 1% of his earnings and 10% of his time for society.

THE FIGHTING WOLVES

An old Cherokee chief was teaching his grandson about life.

"A fight is going on inside me", he said to the boy.

"It is a terrible fight and it is between two wolves."

"One is evil- he is anger, envy, sorrow, regret, greed, arrogance, self pity, guilt, resentment, inferiority, lies, false pride, superiority, self doubt and ego."

"The other is good- he is joy, peace, love, hope, serenity, humility, kindness, benevolence, empathy, generosity, truth, compassion and faith."

"The same fight is going on inside you and inside every other person, too."

The grandson thought about a minute and then asked his grandfather, "Which wolf will win?"

The old chief simply replied, "The one you feed."

17 FEAR

Fear has been mentioned as a vice earlier. However, as in the case of ego, we will have to consider with a balanced and equanimous mind the "fear - as a vice" as well as "fear - as a virtue."

Fear gets generated out of the basic logic of 'desire to live' and 'ego'.

Death is a challenge to the basic logic of desire to live. Fear of death forces a person to tolerate and accept slavery, terrorism, oppression, suppression and exploitation. To what extent one can tolerate or accept it, depends upon the individual as well as on the situation at a particular place, at a particular time. Fear kills the conscience. Sometimes depending on the law and order situation, and social circumstances, one may be constrained to reluctantly tolerate atrocities with fear of death.

Fear has an adverse impact on health. Fear causes sweating, increase in pulse rate, increase in blood pressure, disturbance in endocrinal / hormonal secretions, loss of strength, mental derangements etc. Fright can even kill a person.

Whosoever takes birth, has to die. All living things die one day or the other. That is the law of nature. One must have faith in himself as well as on his future. Death is natural. When the situation arises, the circumstances lead to inevitable death. There is no point in fearing death and affecting one's living.

Fear of death sometimes serves as a boon. Fear of death gives us advance information about impending danger and alerts us-or for that matter all animals or living beings to get rid of danger either by equipping ourselves to fight it out or to run away to safety!

The other basic logic of ego imparts the fear of insult, humiliation, malice, ostracisation by society, failure, defeat, uncertainty etc. This fear is sometimes so grave that it may supersede the basic logic of 'desire to live' and the person is led to suicide!

The worst part of fear is vengeance of an imaginary God or Goddess that not only leads to blind faith but forces a person to lose his money, property and most importantly logical and scientific thinking.

Sometimes one does not notice that he is being deceived. Imaginary concepts of life after death, hell and heaven further add to fear.

The darkness of fear and blind faith is cleared by light of knowledge and scientific and logical approach. If fear knocks at the door, open it with self confidence, there will be none! Fear must have taken to its heels! A coward fears the death and death fears the brave.

There is no better friend than 'fear the virtue' to impart discipline, achieve high standards of morality, etiquettes and manners. If you look at fear in proper perspective it may help you to develop virtues and eliminate vices. Nobody is superior, nobody is inferior and nobody is equal either. People are simply unique and incomparable.

STOP COMPARING YOURSELF

One of the most crippling fears we have is that of not measuring up. Perhaps you feel you won't impress others because they are more confident, successful, intelligent or attractive than you. Such thinking is misguided. The secret of doing well with others is accepting yourself as you are.

This is story about a student, who kept a diary filled with private memories. Some were painful recollections from childhood when he felt hurt, confused, lonely and insecure. He had described fragments of dreams and intensely personal feelings of anger and hatred, as well as things he enjoyed such as Magic shops and coin dealers.

Then a terrible thing happened. After dinner one night he realized that he had left his diary in the cloakroom outside the campus dinning hall. Terrified that somebody might read it and find out the truth about him, he raced back, only to discover that it was gone.

Weeks passed, and eventually he gave up hope of ever finding it again. A month later, he was hanging up his jacket in the same place when he saw his brown, tattered Diary, just where he had left it. Nervously he flicked through the pages and found that a stranger had written this entry : "I'm a lot like you, only I don't keep a diary, I'm grateful to know there are others like me. I hope things turn out well for you."

Tears came to his eyes. It had never dawned on him that anyone could know his inner feelings and also feel things just like the way he did.

So no matter what, whether you're rich or poor, insecure or outgoing, brilliant or average, attractive or plain-some, there are people like you. Discard your fears of not measuring up, and accept yourself as you are.

TIME

Imagine, there is a bank which credits your account each morning with $ 86.400.-- It carries over no balance from day to day. Every evening it deletes whatever part of balance you failed to use during the day. What do you do? DRAW ALL OF IT OF COURSE!

Each one of us has such bank. Its name is 'time'. Every morning it credits you with 86400 seconds. Every night it writes off, as lost, whatever you have failed to invest for good purpose. It carries no balance. It carries no overdraft. If you fail to use the days deposit, loss is yours. There is no going back. There is no drawing against tomorrow.

You must live in the present on today's deposits. Invest it so as to get utmost in Health. Happiness and success. The clock is running. Make the most of today. Remember time waits for no one.

Yesterday is a history.
Tomorrow is a mystery.
Today is a gift.
That's why it is called as 'present'.

18 FAITH

Faith enforced by reason is trust.

The word "Faith" or "Belief" means blind faith or superstition only.To indicate faith, which is not blind, normally the words "Trust", "Assurance' or "Confidence" are used.

Faith is intellectual bankruptcy. Faith is a belief without proof, without reason, without explanation, Faith is a quality which enables us to believe that we know is untrue! Accepting untrue, unscientific, illogical matters is blind faith or superstition which leads one to follow meaningless customs,traditions, and ritual.

The man of science has learnt to believe by experiments, observations, reasoning, justification, verification and logical inference.

Optimism is will power that gives one hope and confidence in one's own abilities which enable him/her to accomplish any task using knowledge, skill, experience and hard-work. There is no need of faith.

Famous Indian social reformer Gopal Ganesh Agarkar (Born :- 15th July 1856 Death:- 17th June 1895, First editor of News paper Kesari, Co-founder of Deccan education society, second Principal of Fergussion College, Pune) has expressed his views on blind faith 125 years ago, as summarised below.

1) Be rational.
2) Improper traditions,foolish religious beliefs, cruel customs and obsolete traditions should be abolished.
3) All traditions,customs and rituals should be critically analysed and verified on principles of humanity before acceptance.
4) Root of establishing religious ideas lies in ignorance,fear, inquisitiveness and desire for safety.
5) A tradition is very old and has lasted over generations is no proof of it's being accurate and good for humanity.
6) Compassion,Benevolence, Truthfulness and equanimity are universally accepted ethics.

7) Don't waste your life on imaginary concepts of heaven and hell.
8) Concepts of "Nationalism" and "Patriotism" are welcome but its excess leading to "Chauvinism" to be avoided.
9) 'Ancient period was "Golden Age" and we should bring it back", is principally unacceptable. According to principles of evolution journey of the human being is from primitive ignorant stage of ancient period to developed, progressed stage today, if at all "Golden Age" exists it will be in future.

Indian freedom fighter and great philosopher Vinayak Damodar Savarkar's views on blind faith and superstition expressed over 100 years ago are expressed below.

1) It is better to help a needy human being than considering cow as holy and helping the animal.
2) Prayer is a hope of human not guarantee of fulfilling the hopes.Repeatedly reading old mythological scriptures do not yield any fruitful results.
3) Vengeance of GOD is ignorance based concept. All rituals to avoid vengeance are meaningless and useless.
4) GOD rushes to help his devotees are fictions from mythology, In reality one has to protect himself or herself.
5) Customs,traditions and rituals which are not at all beneficial to mankind but in fact have nuisance value should be abolished.
6) All books and rituals connected with planet worship should be totally discarded.
7) Instead of donating to so called holy people donate to orphanages for babies,ladies and students.

The views expressed by Agarkar and Savarkar over 100 years back are worth following even today.

Based on comments made by Pandit Mahadeoshastri Divekar in 1946, some common superstitions are given below.

(i) Good omen/Bad omen- The whole world is obsessed with these concepts though they may vary from place to place. What is considered a bad omen in one part of the world may be considered as a good omen in another part of the world e.g. sight of an owl is considered as bad omen by Indians but good omen by some Europeans. A new vehicle is purchased by a person, and subsequently he gains in his business, then it is a lucky vehicle and it is a good omen. In case he loses in the business after purchase of a vehicle, it is considered an unlucky one. This is applied even to human beings in one's life such as wife, son in law, daughter in law and even birth of a child!

If a cat crosses your road, you are finished! It is a very bad omen. If a crow caws in the morning it is bad omen. If you spot a lark, it is an excellent omen, prosperity awaits you! If you yawn, if you sneeze, if you cough, if your eyelid flatters, it is either a good or a bad omen!

If it is a bad omen, remedies are available with the smart 'godmen' who will advise you measures which definitely lead to their prosperity!

Good and bad omens are all games of weak minded people due to blind faith and lack of scientific and logical thinking.

(ii) Auspicious time or day or date- The moment you start any good practice that is the right time to do it. The moment one wants to start a new business, start a long journey, buy a new vehicle, enter a new house, he starts looking for an auspicious time. Can buses and trains in metropolitan cities leave for their destinations at auspicious time? Not at all! Buses, trains and planes have to leave as per the schedule the world over and not by trying to meet auspicious day, date and time! Everyday thousands of vehicles get manufactured the world over. Can you choose auspicious time, auspicious chassis number, auspicious engine number etc.? No! But still when people go for registration of the vehicle they pay heavily for getting auspicious vehicle number!

(iii) Dreams- Dreams reflect your mind. Memories with lingering thoughts and imaginations add up and result in dream. Many times due to mix up of memory and imagination dreams appear altogether different and unknown.

Many a time people give false impression of having dreams without actually having dreams. Sometimes Gods appear in dreams. Obviously a Hindu will dream of Hindu God and a Parsee will see Ahura Mazda! The God gives divine message in such dreams. Then one can collect a bunch of henchmen and a bunch of persons with blind faith and have an excellent business as a "Guru" or "Godman" blessed by the Almighty.

Dreams are natural. To believe in dreams is a blind faith. To claim of having dreams, falsely is cheating.

If one works hard for 8 hours a day and follows good words, good deeds, good thoughts the moment he touches his back to his bed he would be fast-asleep and will not have "such" dreams.

(iv) Ghosts- Legends, gossip, tradition and the imaginary concept of life after death generate ghosts. As mentioned earlier it is believed that after death unsatisfied souls roam around in the form of ghosts. Further hundreds of concepts based on stories, hearsay and gossip get developed. These imaginary ghosts make some leave their beautiful houses, their farms and fields, and search for *tantriks* who advise some rituals and *mantriks* who usher some holy verses to get rid of ghosts. As illiteracy and lack of education is getting eradicated, ghosts are getting lost. Efforts of Dr. Kovoor of Srilanka and many others have scientifically and logically proved that ghosts do not exist. Let us forget about imaginary concept of life after death, ghost, soul, rebirth, etc. leading to blind faith.

(v) Planets and fortunes of humans- Planets Mercury, Venus, Mars, Jupiter, Saturn. Uranus, Pluto, Neptune as well as our natural satellite moon may be influencing the earth due to their gravitational and electromagnetic forces. Is it possible to effect even infinitesimally small change in these forces by wearing some gems or uttering some verses or carrying out some rituals? If planet thousands of kilometer away can effect and influence a human being then a jumbojet or a train or a huge ship will definitely have more effect considering that the forces are proportional to the mass and inversely proportional to the square of the distance. So such ideas of influence of star are absurd, illogical and unscientific.

The experts world over have not been able to formulate and prove any rules or laws of palmistry or horoscopy or astrology with adequate verification. Isolated cases are given as a proof! If you see the "stars foretell" or "fortune" columns in various news papers under the same zodiac sign there will be diametrically opposite remarks.

Let us not get into a wretched state by sinking ourselves in the mud of astrology, horoscope and palmistry!

(vi) Incarnation- Almost every religion considers some of the great human beings as incarnation of God or son of a God or a prophet.

Time creates its own man. Depending on the circumstances, political, social and religious conditions very extraordinary persons rise to the occasion and their thoughts and philosophy influence people for hundreds of years. Such epoch making human being deserve great respect.

However, it is absolutely proper to put the philosophies of these great persons to the test of logic, science and reason before accepting and putting them into practice. The correct way to pay respect to these people is to put into practice their philosophy after your own scrutiny. The society forgets philosophies of these great people, and only practices rituals to worship and praise these greats, call them reincarnation of God, spread as many stories of their miracles as your imagination can fabricate!

Everything works as per laws of nature. There are no miracles. God itself is an imaginary concept developed to explain mysteries of universe, obviously there is no incarnation of God.

(vii) Deadly Consequences- Stories are spread in news papers, magazines, books and even by sending individual letters or handbills about the miracles and change of fortunes experienced by following certain rituals or by being a part of the chain to distribute handbill or send letters. Those who did as per the instructions of rituals got promoted in their service, or flourished in their business. etc and those who did not follow fell sick or died or lost their kiths and kin! The dreadful consequences of not falling in line are so horrible that the fear generated in the mind of some people forces them to reluctantly follow the instructions. Unfortunately, the laws in the country can not catch these culprits and put them to severe punishment. The atmosphere of fear and uncertainty created in society by such people calls for severe punishment.

(viii) Vows in front of deities- Some people have habit of swearing or vowing in front of deities that they will offer him or her something if their desires are fulfilled. They pretend that they have tremendous faith in the deity but their attitude and language itself shows that they do not have faith in deity. "Let my son pass his examinations in flying colours and I will give you one kilograms of sweets!"

There is no advance paid! The deity is not believed even for the amount worth cost of 1kg. of sweets! It is bribing. The deity is considered corrupt! Deity will do something only if you bribe! This is ridiculous superstition.

LIFE'S LESSON

This is the story of a donkey that fell into a well. He cried and cried but no one saved him. The farmer who owned him felt that it was pointless to save the donkey because it was old and useless. Since the well was dry anyway, he decided to fill it up with soil so that the well would get filled up and the donkey would be buried. He therefore called his neighbors to help him fill up the well. As they started throwing soil in the well, the donkey realized what was happening and cried even more. Just a little later, everyone was surprised that the donkey was no longer crying. The farmer looked inside to see what was happening. He was surprised that each time the soil was thrown in and it fell on the donkey, it would shake off the soil and climb on top of the hill that was being made. Soon, to the astonishment of everyone, the donkey managed to step out of the well.

The conclusion is that life will throw all kinds of garbage and stones on you. You just have to learn to shake them off. Each stone that is thrown at you should be looked on as a stepping stone for progressing-nothing should stop you- not even the deepest of the wells.

19 TOLERANCE, RESTRAINT, PATIENCE

Bigotry, fanaticism, bloodshed and brutality must stop. Persecution in the name of blasphemy must stop. Tolerant society has no place for this.

Tolerance means respecting the thoughts, value system and religion of others. Tolerance is essential to maintain good relations on individual, social and interstate levels. Any difference of opinions are to be settled with mutual discussion or to agree to have different opinions and accept the situation. Belligerent attitude, animosity has to be avoided. Expecting that your views and opinions will be accepted by all and try to force your views on others is intolerance. Reality must be accepted.

Our friends, relatives, collegues make mistakes, knowingly or unknowning. Tolerance teaches us to liberally and benevolently pardon them and bear the consequences of the mistakes courageously and open heartedly. Tolerance does not mean surrender or to calmly bear the injustice but magnanemously accept the reality and boldly face it. Tolerance teaches us to bear the adverse comments against us. Tolerance teaches us to calmly listen to thoughts of others which may not be acceptable or agreeable to us. It teaches us to agree to disagree calmly.

16th November is declared as International Tolerance day.

In life nothing happens instantaneously. It takes time. You can't get a chicken by smashing an egg but you have to allow appropriate time to hatch the egg. You can't built muscles overnight. You have to exercise and take proper diet to built your muscles for months. You need patience perseverance and hard work. You have to wait without frustration, without complaining, calmly- that is patience.

Ailments, pain, illness are inevitable. Everytime everything can not happen as per your wishes, as per your expectations or in your favour. To face such situations bravely, calmly, patiently is endurance. 'What can not be cured, must be endured.'

The people without endurance, without patience, without

tolerance neither live peacefully nor allow others to live peacefully.

In society, you have to live along with a wide variety of people. If you have altruistic attitude, you think of others and live peacefully. In unfavourable conditions such people keep their cool and are 'ideal' for society. Every one may not be able to reach that status. But with firm will power and determination, one can learn to live calmly in adverse situation by increasing one's endurance.

The worse part of impatient, intolerant and consequently indisciplined people is that they loose civic sense. The simple disciplines taught in civics at school level are forgotten e.g.

* Stand in Q at bus stop.
* Stand in Q at cinema theaters, match tickets.
* If traffic jam is there do not overtake and block the traffic from opposite direction.
* Follow signals where ever signals are there otherwise 'stop and proceed' at every crossing.
* Follow speed limit.
* Do not honk unnecessarily.
* Do not overtake unnecessarily.
* Change the lanes only when necessary by using left right indicators.

Haste is waste.

Retraint teaches humanity. Keeps desires of your senses and temptations of your mind undercontrol. Your thoughts behaviour and emotions are controlled. Good words good deeds, good thoughts, discipline, conscience, sensitivity and joy are natural outcome from restraint. It has positive effect on body. You get freedom from anger, belligerance, regret. You build health. Take care that you do not hurt anybody not just physically but mentally as well. Avoid abusing, insulting, rebuking anybody.

Without restraint one loses mental balance. Their is no control over your desires and temptations. You move towards crime. Atrocities, violence, adultry, gambling, addictions results. Lack of restraint leads to criminal and immoral behaviour.

LAW OF THE GARBAGE TRUCK

One day I hopped in a taxi and we took off for the airport.
We were driving in the right lane when suddenly a black car
jumped out of a parking space right in front of us.
My taxi driver slammed on his brakes, skidded,
and missed the other car by just inches!
The driver of the other car whipped
his head around and started yelling at us.
My taxi driver just smiled and waved at the guy.
And I mean, he was really friendly.
So I asked, 'Why did you just do that? This guy almost ruined
your car and sent us to the hospital!'

This is when my taxi driver taught me what I now call,
'The Law of the Garbage Truck.'

He explained that many people are like garbage trucks.
They run around full of garbage, full of frustration,
full of anger, and full of disappointment.
As their garbage piles up, they need a place to dump it
and sometimes they'll dump it on you.
Don't take it personally.

Just smile, wave, wish them well, and move on.
Don't take their garbage and spread it to other people
at work, at home, or on the streets.

The bottom line is that successful people do not let
garbage trucks take over their day.
Life's too short to wake up in the morning with regrets,
so... Love the people who treat you right.
Pray for the ones who don't.

Life is ten percent what you make it
and ninety percent how you take it!

Have a garbage-free 2 day and 2 morrow and everyday!

20 RESPECT / HONOUR

Respect is to hold in esteem or honour.

Ego is the basic logic. Not to disturb the ego of others is to give respect. If you get freedom from your ego, you can be modest, you can be lenient, you can respect others.

We respect persons who are our idols. We respect persons who are honoured by the society, who have excelled in one field or the other, who are famous. Fame is the fragrance of good deeds. We normally respect all such people without hesitation. The real virtue is to respect other human beings, even if they are younger than you or at a much lower cadre than you as far as economic, educational and social status is concerned. The one who has got rid of 'ego-the vice' and developed modesty; the one who knows what he owes society, the one who is full of gratitude to others who form the society, can only respect others.

Treat every human being with humanity. Respect and value time of others - it is as valuable to them as it is to you. Respect other's opinions. Respect freedom of others.

In order to respect others, one should avoid the following.

(1)   Abhorrence.
(2)   Jealousy.
(3)   Insult.
(4)   Ridicule
(5)   Reprimand
(6)   Envy.
(7)   Hatred.
(8)   Prejudice.
(9)   Judgement.
(10) Adamance.
(11) Advice.
(12) Terrorism.
(13) Unnecessary sympathy.

In order to show respect to others one should not forget to
(1)   Express thanks
(2)   Express good wishes.
(3)   Express blessings to the young.
(4)   Congratulate
(5)   Appreciate
(6)   Value the time of others
(7)   Respond quickly
(8)   Have mutual understanding
(9)   Empathise
(10) Use soft language

Your status will not go down by respecting others. Command respect, do not demand respect.

WOODEN BOWL

A frail old man went to live with his son, daughter-in-law, and four-year old grandson. The old man's hands trembled, his eyesight was blurred, and his step faltered. The family ate together at the table. But the elderly grandfather's shaky hands and failing sight made eating difficult. Peas rolled off his spoon onto the floor. When he grasped the glass, milk spilled on the tablecloth. The son and daughter-in-law became irritated with the mess.

"We must do something about Grandfather," said the son. "I've had enough of his spilled milk, noisy eating, and food on the floor." So the husband and wife set a small table in the corner.

There, Grandfather ate alone while the rest of the family enjoyed dinner. Since Grandfather had broken a dish or two, his food was served in a wooden bowl.

When the family glanced in Grandfather's direction, sometime he has a tear in his eye as he sat alone. Still, the only words the couple had for him were sharp admonitions when he dropped a fork or spilled food.

The four-year-old watched it all in silence. One evening before supper, the father noticed his son playing with wood scraps on the floor. He asked the child sweetly, "What are you making?" Just as sweetly, the boy responded, "Oh, I am making a little bowl for you and Mama to eat your food when I grow up." The four-year-old smiled and went back to work.

The words so struck the parents that they were speechless. Then tears started to stream down their cheeks. Though no word was spoken, both knew what must be done.

That evening the husband took Grandfather's hand and gently led him back to the family table. For the remainder of his days he ate every meal with the family. And for some reason, neither husband nor wife seemed to care any longer when a fork was dropped, milk spilled, or the tablecloth soiled.

Care and love your Parents as you would expect your children to love and care for you.

Remember as you sow, so shall you reap. Regardless of your relationship with your parents, you will miss them when they are gone.

21 POPULATION

Population explosion is the biggest problem of human race as it entered the 21st century with a population of around 6000 millions.

In the 16th century this planet was inhabited by just 500 million human beings, the 20th century began with 1650 million, and now we are 7900 million in 2021!

Consider the size of our planet. It is covered by water over 71% of its area. Out of 29% area covered by land, the area covered by snow, mountains, deserts, marshes, dense forests etc are unsuitable for habitation. The space required by human beings for the following need to be considered
*   Residence to live,
*   To grow crops, to grow fruits, to grow vegetables
*   Pastures for cattle, sheep, goats to graze
*   Water supply systems comprising dams, lakes, rivers, canals, pumping stations, water purification plants
*   Transportation of human beings and goods—roads, railways, airports, metros, bus stations, railway stations, --automobile industry to manufacture trucks, trailers, tankers, buses, cars,--aero plane manufacture, shipping industry to make ships, boats for transport as well as fishing,
*   Educational institutions—schools, colleges, universities
*   Industries like mining, engineering, information technology, cement, sugar, textile, food processing, electrical white goods etc.
*   Commercial activities like banking, insurance, storage and marketing of all the items required by human beings from different walks of life
*   Power generation—hydal, atomic, solar, wind energy based and its distribution
*   Health requirements such as hospitals, dispensaries,

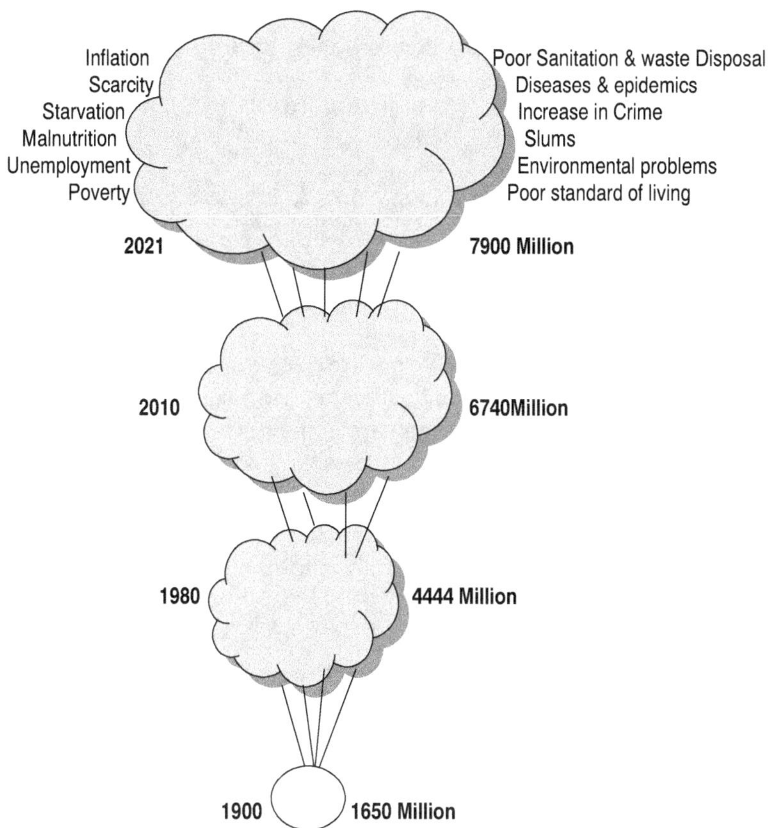

Population Explosion

pharmaceutical industries to manufacture medicines and their distribution system

•   Safety, security and administrative needs such as army, police, fire brigade, legislature and executive system to form and run the Government and the country, judicial system etc.

•   Social, political and religious activities

How many people can live comfortably on this planet with peaceful co-existence with other flora and fauna? Probably to live peacefully, without scarcity and wants of minimum basic needs, the human population on this planet needs to be restricted to 1980   level of 4444 million.

Over population have the following results:

1)   Scarcity of basic needs food, water and shelter resulting in starvation, malnutrition, overcrowded living

2)   Enormous demands and depleting supplies results in spiraling up of prices

3)   Hygienic conditions deteriorate, sewage disposal/sanitation, waste disposal becomes unmanageable, infectious diseases, epidemics and pandemics create chaos.

4)   Unemployment increases, poverty increases.

5)   Adulteration of food and drugs, contamination of water, air pollution, noise pollution soil contamination increase

6)   Increase in crime, addiction gambling and unrest results in increase in social tension

7)   Environmental problems increase

8)   Survival of flora and fauna is affected

9)   Benefits of progress and development of human race over thousands of years are lost

10) Standard of living deteriorates

11) Safety and peace of human beings is at stake

11th July is population awareness day. Unfortunately the political, social and religious leaders- the world over—have not paid due attention to this grave problem which basically endangers the very existence and survival of human race on this planet .Even today, over
7 million people died in2020 for want of adequate drinking water and food!

Population reduction will not only benefit the entire mankind or the country but even if you think on individual and family basis, your child can have better food, clothes, shelter, education, and health facilities, if you restrict your family. The child can receive full attention of its parents as needed psychologically.

Obsession for male child is one of the major causes of today's negligence towards family planning. The great women who have led their countries---Sri Lanka, India, U K,-Pakistan, Bangladesh, Myanmar, Germany, Israel, Australia, .Norway etc would definitely inspire generations to get rid of gender discrimination and obsession for male child.

Let us review some basics regarding population.

Census- It is counting of the population of the country after certain pre-determined period (Say 10 years) by every country.
Birth rate- It is average number of births per year per 1000 people.
Fertility Rate-It is average number of child births per woman during her life time.
Death Rate- It is average number of deaths per 1000 people per year.
Infant Mortality rate- It is number of infants dying before reaching one year of age per 1000 live births per year.
Life Expectancy- It is the average life-span of a child at the time of birth depending on the average age of death in that area/country expecting that the conditions remain unchanged.

When the birth rate is higher than the death rate the population increases and when birth rate is less than the death rate the population decreases.

Life expectancy depends on the availability of air, water, food, shelter, clothing, health facilities and their condition as well as mental set up due to social and economic conditions.
Death rate depends on life expectancy as well as age distribution in the area under consideration.
Birth rate depends on children per family and age distribution
The present (2021) world death rate is 7.61 as per the figures available on the internet. If the population has to be reduced then the birth rate has to be lower than the world death rate of 7.61.

How do we go about to tackle and resolve the problem? It is possible if one couple one child policy is adopted and successfully executed. This means fertility rate of one. The fertility rate being independent of life expectancy and age distribution it is the most accurate indicator of population status. The populations of countries having population more than 50 million, their birth rate, fertility rate, life expectancy are given in the table below based on 2020 data available on the internet.

Sl no	Country	Population Millions	Birth rate	Fertility rate	Life Expectancy	Death rate
1	China	1439	12.3	1.7	77.47	7.26
2	India	1380,	19	2.2	70.42	7.27
3	U S	331	12.5	1.3	79.11	8.78
4	Indonesia	273	16.2	2.3	72.32	6.51
5	Brazil	212	4.1	1.7	76.57	6.5
6	Pakistan	221	21.9	3.6	67.79	6.93
7	Nigeria	206	36.9	5.4	55.75	11.77
8	Bangladesh	165	18.8	2.1	73.57	5.54
9	Russia	146	11	1.8	72.94	12.79
10	Japan	126	7.7	1.4	85.03	10.65
11	Mexico	129	18.3	2.1	75.41	6.04
12	Philippines	110	23.7	2.6	71.66	5.9
13	Vietnam	97	15.5	2.1	75.77	6.35
14	Germany	84	8.6	1.6	81.86	11.28
15	Ethiopia	115	36.5	4.3	67.81	6.53
16	Egypt	102	29.6	3.3	72.54	5.81
17	Iran	84	17.9	2.2	77.33	4.87
18	Turkey	84	15.7	2.1	78.45	5.44
19	Dem Congo	89	34.4	6	61.6	9.41
20	Thailand	70	11	1.5	77.74	7.75
21	France	65	12.2	1.9	83.13	9.32
22	U K	68	12.1	1.8	81.77	9.4
23	Italy	60	8.6	1.3	84.01	10.57
24	Myanmar	54	18.1	2.2	67.78	8.24
25	South Africa	59	20.2	2.4	64.88	9.49
26	South Korea	51	8.3	1.1	83.5	6.11
27	World	7828	17.89	2.45	70.8	7.612

In 20 years population can increase by 50% but it takes over 80 years and tremendous efforts to reduce the population by just 10% and this is the biggest problem and challenge which must be understood and acted upon.

I WILL TELL YOU WHY

Air is polluted,
Water is contaminated
Food is adultrated
I will tell you why
Because of population Explosion
From 1980 to 2016
From4450 millions to 7450 millions

Scarcity of food
Scarcity of water
Scarcity of shelter
Scarcity of employment
I will tell you why
Because of population explosion

Flora and Fawna are in danger
Many animals getting extinct
Many plants likely to vanish
Ecological imbalance has shattered earth
I will tell you why
Because of population explosion

Corruption is on rise
Adultration is on rise
Addiction is on rise
Gambling is on rise
I will tell you why
Because of population explosion

Rise people rise,Fight population Explosion
One Man One wife, One Family One child
Let us go back to 1980 population
I will tell you why
To make this planet a better place to live.

22 SPORTS AND SPORTSMANSHIP

As mankind moves from belligerence to peaceful coexistence and as society moves from religious fanaticism to realistic, logical and scientific attitude, the time spent for activities of war and religious rituals will be freely available. This time can be best utilized to improve the psychological and physical condition of human beings through sports.

Sports and sportsmanship is an inherent part of today's civilization to maintain and improve physical and mental health of individual as well as society.

Athletics, football, hockey, cricket, badminton and tennis are slowly becoming global. In 2021,Tokyo Olympics 2020 were conducted with one year delay due to Covid19 pademic.11656 athlete of 206 countries participated in 339 events in 33 sports. The whole world was charged with enthusiasm. The feeling of oneness of mankind pervaded the globe. Everyone felt as if it was his or her competition. The same thing happens during world cup football or hockey tournaments or Wimbledon Tennis Tournament. The feeling of involvement pervades the world.

Further these sports competitions give real pleasure and happiness not only to those who participate but thousands who witness these games at site and millions who see the games on television. From a year old to a hundred years old, the disabled to able, the sick to the healthy all can enjoy watching the sports events. With the state of the art technology you can watch any international event live. Sports has really contributed in bringing the world together as one family.

Motto of all sports competitions is "better than the best". Sports encourages people to continuously strive for the better, continuously strive to improve. The Olympic motto is "CITUS-ALTIUS-FORTIUS" -FASTER HIGHER and STRONGER.

Sportsmanship typically represents component of morality in sports and helps human beings to live in the competitive world maintaining fairness, ethics, respect and "fellowship" with one's competitors.

Sportsmanship gives you ability to accept defeat smilingly and accept victory modestly.

Fair play refers to all participants having an equitable chance to pursue victory and acting towards others in an honest, straight forward and dignified manner, even though one may feel injustice or unfairness from team members, other competitors, opponents, umpires or officials.

Character refers to dispositions, values and habits that determine the way that person responds to desires, fears, challenges, opportunities, failures and successes in sports as well as in life.

Nothing else has succeeded in developing fraternity or global brotherhood like sports.

Unfortunately some unwanted elements crop up due to aggressive and excessive nationalism and defeats in sports sometimes results in riots, fights, abhorrence and hatred. The power of sports to develop brotherhood and affection should never be allowed to be overcome by feeling of emotions of vengeance and hatred.

Gambling in sports should be completely prohibited. Some countries have horse races like athletics without betting!

Competition has become inevitable part of today's life. Healthy competition is essential. Without competition laziness, dullness, inefficiency and mediocracy flourishes. Excellence, intelligence, proficiency, skill, ability, competence, endurance come out from competition. There is continuous improvement, a search for better than the best.

If competitions are not healthy and do not follow strict rules and regulations and discipline that lead to fair and equal opportunity to all, impartial treatment to all, the competitions would lead to injustice and enmity. Mental tensions, worry and safety problem may get generated.

Sports and sportsmanship teach us the spirit of healthy competitions.

Let us patronize sports.

Fundamental Principles of Olympism

1. Olympism is a philosophy of life, exalting and combining in a balanced whole the qualities of body, will and mind. Blending sport with culture and education, Olympism seeks to create a way of life based on the joy of effort, the educational value to good example and respect for universal fundamental ethical principles.
2. The goal of Olympism is to place sport at the service of the harmonious development of man, with a view to promoting a peaceful society concerned with the preservation of human dignity.
3. The Olympic Movement is the concerted, organized, universal and permanent action, carried out under the supreme authority of the IOC, of all individuals and entities who are inspired by the values of Olympism. It covers the five continents. It reaches its peak with the bringing together of the world's athletes at the great sports festival, the Olympic Games. Its symbol is five interlaced rings.
4. The practice of sport is a human right. Every individual must have the possibility of practising sport, without discrimination of any kind and in the Olympic spirit, which requires mutual understanding with a spirit of friendship, solidarity and fair play. The organization, administration and management of sport must be controlled by independent sports organizations.
5. Any form of discrimination with regard to a country or a person on grounds of race, religion, politics, gender or otherwise is incompatible with belonging to the Olympic Movement.
6. Belonging to the Olympic Movement requires compliance with the Olympic Charter and recognition by the IOC.

SCARS OF ANGER

There once was a little boy who had a bad temper. His father gave him a bag of nails and told him that every time he lost his temper, he must hammer a nail into the back of the fence. Over the next few weeks, as he learned to control his anger, the number of nails hammered daily gradually dwindled down. He discovered it was easier to hold his temper than to drive those nails in the fence. Finally the day came when the boy didn't lose his temper at all. He told his father about it and the father suggested that the boy now pull out one nail for each day that he was able to hold his temper. The days passed and the young boy was finally able to tell his father that all the nails were gone.

The father took his son by the hand and led him to the fence. He said, "You have done well, my son, but look at the holes in the fence. The fence will never be the same. When you say things in anger, they leave a scar just like this one." A verbal wound is as bad as a physical one.

Anger not only leaves a verbal wound, but also leaves a major physical aliment. It is a known medical fact that when you are Angry, your entire system gets a severe jolt, just like an earth-quake. Numerous people have had massive heart attacks when they were angry. Some died, some survived and some got paralyzed.

So let's try to cage and contain this Anger, if not for any-one else, for our own-self.

23 ADDICTION

Some substances after entering the human body affect the brain and the nervous system. One gets habituated to the feeling of numbness and lightness often referred to as a 'kick'. The habit of getting kick from these substances, known as toxicants, is called as addiction. Mankind has developed several addictions which can be broadly classified into three categories.

(1) Taking tobacco in different forms.

(2) Drinking alcoholic beverages.

(3) Consuming opium, LSD, hemp, "brown sugar" etc. branded as drug addiction.

In most of the countries the third category is legally banned and possession of "drugs", their transport, sale and consumption is considered as a serious offence. Society also condemns this category. However, enough efforts have not been made to scrupulously destroy the drugs, probably due to corruption at administrative, political, religious and law enforcement levels. The high costs and tremendous profitability in the drug business make the people extremely rich, "respectable" and influential people in the society. The individual, group of individuals, society, administration, judiciary and police, social, political and religious leaders should join hands to unveil such bad elements, and strip them of their wealth and status, and punish them severely, so that no one would ever dare to enter such an illegal, immoral business harmful to society. Fortunately these drugs are not openly and prestigiously consumed.

The situation is unfortunate and lamentable about the first two categories. The elite and the famous, the living legends and idols depict alcohol consumption and smoking as a status symbol. We would briefly review the status of these addictions.

To chew tobacco or to inhale smoke of tobacco through cigarette or pipe or cigars, to apply roasted tobacco powder to teeth, inhale flavoured tobacco powder as snuff are the various ways to take tobacco inside the body to give a 'kick'. The world Health

Organization (WHO) has declared 31st May as a tobacco free day. This is only a beginning. Tobacco free day should follow tobacco free week and then tobacco free month and tobacco free year. Ultimately we have to achieve tobacco free life. Finally cultivation of tobacco as a crop should be stopped. This should be done by educating the people about the bad effects of tobacco. Once this is understood, then one will get convinced and change one's mind and consequently cultivation of tobacco can be stopped.

Today thousands of people world over are earning their livelihood on tobacco farming, trading, cigarette manufacture, advertisement and sale. Within a specified period alternative means to earn livelihood should be offered and established. If people unite the world over and make a serious effort to develop suitable profession/trade as substitute to those who depend on tobacco based products for their livelihood, this planet can be 90% free from tobacco in just 10 years!

Taking tobacco in any form is harmful to body.

Let us resolve not to chew tobacco.

Let us resolve not to smoke tobacco.

Let us resolve not to inhale tobacco.

Unfortunately if any of these habits has been developed, one should slowly reduce and finally stop the habit. The idea that the tobacco refreshes and freshens the brain and the nervous system is merely an illusion. In fact tobacco causes interference in the working of the brain and the nervous system, adversely affecting its functioning. The tobacco contains poisonous nicotine and tar. The tar enters the lungs and gets deposited there. Slowly the deposits increase reducing the amount of air inhaled and amount of oxygen supplied to the body. If you take a filtered cigarette, wet it's filter in water and you can open the filter after smoking and observe the tar trapped there. You will never smoke again if you see this tar which normally enters your body with each cigarette smoked.

Smoking in all offices, industries, public gardens, roads, railways and aeroplanes should be prohibited to begin the drive with ultimate aim to stop tobacco consumption totally.

With growing industrialization drinking alcohol is becoming a status sumbol. A party without alcohol is not considered a 'party' at all! Alcoholic addiction is a mental disorder (Dipsomania). It causes physical, psychological, family, social and national damage.

Smoking affects brain and nervous system, respiratory and circulatory system. Alcohol affects all these systems and additionally damages liver and digestive system.

The drinking habit begins as a company to disillusioned friends, to have fun, to enjoy life, to get rid of disgust, sadness, humiliation, worries, anxieties, troubles etc. It is ignorance and lack of knowledge.

"Alcoholic Anonymous" organization is working the world over to eliminate alcoholic addiction and everyone should contribute financially or otherwise to such organizations working for betterment of mankind.

Let us resolve to make the mankind free from addiction, starting from ourselves.

WORK WORK WORK

A long time ago, there was an Emperor who told his horseman that if he could ride on his horse and cover as much land area as he likes, in a day before sunset, then the Emperor would give him the area of land he has encircled.

Sure enough, the horseman quickly jumped onto his horse and rode as fast as possible to cover as much land area as he could. He kept on riding and riding, whipping the horse to go as fast as possible. When he was hungry or tired, he did not stop because he wanted to cover as much area as possible.

Came to a point when he had covered a substantial area and he was exhausted and was dying. Then he asked himself, "Why did I push myself so hard to cover so much land area? Now I am dying and I only need a very small area to bury myself."

The above story is similar with the journey of our life. We push very hard everyday to make more money, to gain power and recognition. We neglect our health, time with our family and to appreciate the surrounding beauty and the hobbies we love.

One day when we look back, we will realize that we don't really need that much, but then we cannot turn back time for what we have missed.

Life is not about making money, acquiring power or recognition. Life is definitely not about work! Work is only necessary to keep us living so as to enjoy the beauty and pleasures of life. Life is a balance of Work and Play, Family and Personal time. You have to decide how you want to balance your Life. Define your priorities, realize what you are able to compromise but always let some of your decisions be based on your instincts. Happiness is the meaning and the purpose of Life, the whole aim of human existence.

So, take it easy, do what you want to do and appreciate nature. Life is fragile, Life is short. Do not take Life for granted. Live a balanced lifestyle and enjoy Life!

Watch your thoughts; they become words.

Watch your words; they become actions.

Watch your actions; they become habits.

Watch your habits; they become character.

Watch your character; it becomes your destiny.

24 GAMBLING / BETTING

Gambling and betting is one of the banes to the mankind, with a long history of over 5000 years. Horse racing, playing cards with heavy stakes and share markets are prestigious gambling dens. Betting worth millions of dollars on forecasting winners of international sports tournaments is recent addition. Greed, selfish motives, and desire to get rich fast without doing any hard work forces people to run after lotteries, betting and horse races etc. Reckless thinking, lack of foresight, improper conditioning of mind lead to this path.

A gambler earns one and loses hundred. No one has ever flourished in life by gambling. Gambling is the fastest way to become poor. There is no gambler who has never cried, never regretted. Loser in gambling gets instigated to gamble till he becomes so poor that he can not buy one time food. Gainer in gambling, again gambles to get more money till he loses all his money as well as his reputation.

Just have a look around. How many rich and famous people around you have achieved their status and created their wealth through gambling and betting and how many people have achieved through hard work, deep thinking, creative and constructive work? If you think a little, gambling is definitely not the right path to follow.

Unfortunately, gambling tendencies are on the rise. Lottery tickets are sold at every nook and corner. Newspapers and televisions advertise day and night for gifts and prizes for lucky numbers, with disproportionately high values. For a purchase worth 100 dollars you are offered a lucky winner prize of 10,000 dollars! Mankind is pulled out from world of realities to world of fantasies and people are being made lazy, shirking from work. Productive, creative and constructive tendencies are destroyed. This paralyses society and makes it inactive.

Let us resolve to eradicate gambling and betting of any sort as is already done in some countries.

FOR THOSE WHO ARE ALWAYS IN A RUSH

A guy was driving at 70 miles in a 40 mile zone, when a cop came behind him with the flashers on. As he parked and stopped, he could see the cop getting out of his car. Right away the guy started thinking of excuses to give, as this was not the first time, he had been in similar situations many times before.

As the cop approached him, he said 'Hi officer, I guess you caught me over the limit little bit, I was in a rush to get home, to be with my wife and kids, you know my younger son wasn't feeling too well, when I left home this morning.'

The cop said, "Well, I guess so", and started scribbling on his pad. As minutes went by, he could see from the side-view mirror, the cop was still scribbling. The guy was wondering why he hadn't asked for his driver's license so far. A few moments later, the cop came to his window and handed him a folded paper, and returned back to his car without saying a single word. The guy started to wonder, how much this ticket is going to be as he began to unfold the paper. He was surprised it was not a ticket as he began to read:

"I had a daughter who was killed by a speeding car at the age of six, by a speeding driver like you. He got a fine, few months in jail, and was free, free to hug his two other daughters. I only had one, and now I can never hug her again. I have tried to forgive that guy a thousand times, and I thought I had. Maybe I really did forgive him, but I have to do it again, even right now. So pray for me, and be careful when you drive again.

The guy was totally dumb-founded and could not move for the next few minutes. When finally he did, he drove slowly, even few miles under the speed limit, praying for forgiveness.

Do not rush in life- It won't take you any-where. Take one day at a time, be the driver of your life within the limits of nature. Betting and gambling is trying to overspeed your vehicle which invites accident.

25 THEFT / STEALING AND CORRUPTION

To steal is a crime world over and to refrain from stealing is a virtue. Wealth accumulated by a person by justifiable means and hard work should become his property. If people are allowed to rob, the tendency to create the wealth by sincere, honest hard work will be hampered and the society or civilization will get shattered.

Theft, however small or negligible, needs appropriate atonement or punishment. Kleptomania is a disorder of mind. Greed, selfishness and temptation lead to theft.

During famine, wars or natural calamities, only to survive, if someone steals food or clothes or medicines it may be pardonable. In all other circumstances, theft is deplorable and punishable, depending on gravity of the situation in each case.

Some people in a society get special authorities/decision making powers due to their position in business, politics, judiciary administration or society. It is their duty to exercise their authority honestly and do justice to their responsibilities.

To get direct or indirect benefits for oneself or his kiths and kins and misuse of power according to these gains is corruption and the gain is called the bribe.

Corruption is a social injustice. It is a cancer to the society. If you start getting excellent marks without studies, you start getting awards without merit, get money without knowledge and efforts, the society will collapse.

Corruption involves minimum two people. One who gives bribe and one who takes bribe. If bribe is not given, there can be no corruption. If a person does not take bribe, the people can't give bribe, and there can be no corruption.

Why a person gives bribe? Invariably he lacks in quality, ability, performance, merit, efforts, hard work. It is to cover up some lacuna or shortcoming, sometimes, in spite of all merits, to save time and avoid unnecessary running around, people give bribe.

Selfish motives, increased temptations and consequently

increased requirements or needs to meet expenses for children's education, daughters marriage, grave illness in family force person to take bribe. To end corruption every individual has to resolve, not to take and not to give bribe.

Honesty

A merchant wanted to purchase a gorgeous camel in the market and after spotting one began to settles for it with the seller. There was a long bargain between the merchant and the camel seller, and finally the merchant bought the camel and took it home. On reaching home, the merchant called his servant to take out the camel's saddle.Under the sadle, the servant found a small velvet bag which upon opening revealed him to be full of precious diamond gems!
The servant shouted, "boss, you bought a camel, but look what came with it for free!"
The merchant was surprised, he saw diamonds in his servant's hands which were shining and twinkling even more in the sunlight.
The merchant said: "i have bought a camel and not the diamonds, i should return it immediately."
The servant was thinking in his mind "how stupid my boss is ...!"
He said: "nobody will know who the owner is!" However, the merchant did not listen to him and immediately reached the market and returned the velvet bag to the shopkeeper.
The camel seller was very happy, said, "i had forgotten that i had hidden my precious stones under the sadle.
Now you choose any one diamond as a reward!
The merchant said, "i have paid the right price for the camel so i do not need any gift and prizes!"

The more the merchant was refusing, the more the camel seller was insisting.

Finally, the merchant smiled and said," in fact, when i decided to bring back the bag, i had already kept two of the most precious diamonds with me."

After this confession, the camel seller was infuriated and he quickly emptied the bag and began to count his diamond gems.
After he counted the diamonds, with a heavy sigh of relief, he said "these are all my diamonds, so what were the two most precious ones that you kept?"
The merchant said,*"my honesty and my self-respect."
The seller was dumb-struck!
We have to look within ourselves to find out if we possess any of these 2 diamonds.
Anyone who has these 2 diamonds, honesty and self-respect, is the richest person in the world.

ART

The productive, creative and constructive abilities of humans manifest as art.

The human mind is continuously at work. It requires some relaxation. It requires some rest. A hobby is necessary to provide rest and relaxation. Art provides the need of this hobby, diverts the mind from leaning toward destructive tendencies. Arts relieve worries and tensions.

Singing, dancing, playing various musical instruments, drawing and painting, creating sculptures, acting in dramas, movies etc. are the arts that give happiness, pleasure, unity and mutual goodwill. Art knows no bounds. It is global. Excellence in art is globally appreciated irrespective of caste, creed, race, religion and nationality of the artist. Artists have great influence on society which can be utilized to improve mutual understanding.

Cultivation of art and patronizing art is the responsibility of every civilized human.

THE CARPENTER

An elderly carpenter was ready to retire. He told his employer-contractor of his plans to leave the house- building business and live a more leisurely life with his wife enjoying his extended family. He would miss the paycheck, but he needed to retire. They could get by.

The contractor was sorry to see his good worker go and asked if he could build just one more house as a personal favor. The carpenter said yes, but in time it was easy to see that his heart was not in his work. He resorted to shoddy workmanship and --- inferior materials. It was an unfortunate way to end a dedicated career.

When the carpenter finished his work the employer came to inspect the house. He handed the front-door key to the carpenter.

"This is your house," he said, "my gift to you."

The carpenter was shocked! What a shame!

If he had only known he was building his own house, he would have done it all so differently.

So it is with us. We build our lives, a day at a time, often putting less than our best into the building. Then with a shock we realize we have to live in the house we have built. If we could do it over, we'd do it much differently. But we cannot go back.

You are the carpenter. Each day you hammer a nail, place a board, or erect a wall. "Life is a do-it-yourself project," someone has said. Your attitudes and the choices you make today, build the "house" you live in tomorrow. Build wisely!

In pursuance of excellence is the motto. Whatever you do try to do as best as you can.

27 KNOWLEDGE

Knowledge is facts, information, skills acquired through experience and education.It is theoretical and practical understanding and comprehension of the subject. It is awareness or familiarity gained by experience and education of a fact or situation. It is sum of what is known.

Lack of knowledge is ignorance. In no time of human history ignorance was better than knowledge.

Wisdom is use of knowledge, with judgement.

Prudence is application of knowledge carefully and discretely, foreseeing and avoiding undesired consequences and risks.

Laws of nature is science. To understand the laws of nature is knowledge. Without trying to understand the laws of nature arguments raised through intellectual circus is lack of knowledge.

To know the truth, facts, reality is knowledge. Curiosity, capacity to think and ponder, research and analyse leads human society to fact finding and gaining knowledge.

Physics, chemistry and biology are the basic sciences. No one can claim to have full knowledge or proficiency even of one of these sciences, leave aside of total laws of nature. However, to have scientific approach is most important and every civilized human should have a scientific approach. It involves keen observations, logical thinking, postulation of hypothesis, conducting experiments for verification of hypothesis and arriving at inferences. Everything should be open and transparent. (Glasnost and Perestroika).

Knowledge should be utilized for the benefit of mankind and other flora and fauna. Knowledge should be utilized to achieve better availability of basic needs of food, clothing, shelter, health and education and finally reach the goal of safe, peaceful, happy and contented life.

In 20th century, there were tremendous improvements in the availability of basic needs. Crops, fruits and vegetable production not only increased in quantity but qualitatively as well. Mankind did not have availability of so much of potable water ever before. Radio, television, telephone, telefaxes, satellite communication have revolutionized communication through knowledge of laws of nature. Science provided tremendous availability of energy from mineral oils and electricity. Computers provided speed and accuracy that was never dreamt of. Artificial fibre and plastics provided so many utility goods. Transport by air, sea and road was revolutionized by aeroplanes, helicopters, hover crafts, large cruisers, motor cars, trucks, motorcycles and scooters.

Standard of living improved tremendously. Electricity helped to provide so many consumer goods. Lamps and fluorescent tubes revolutionized living. Vacuum cleaners, washing machines, microwave ovens, mixers, food processors, refrigerators made daily routine more comfortable. Unfortunately explosion of population from 1600 million to 6000 million in 20th century alone did not allow mankind to enjoy full benefit of the development and progress. Scarcity and want could not be eliminated.

Lack of proper knowledge led to wrong concept and blind faith. Religion instead of giving philosophy of life provided philosophy of dead! Religion failed to improve individual and social morality and harmony in the society through mutual trust and understanding. Crime spread unabated. Gains of science were lost.

Improved knowledge of human mind, its nature and working need to be utilized to develop benevolent human being with a high standard of morality. Let us resolve to learn from the mistakes of the past.

Courage is a special kind of knowledge, the knowledge of how to fear what ought to be feared and how not to fear what ought not to be feared.

Learn from the mistakes of others, you can't live long enough to make them all yourself.

Learning and innovation go hand in hand.

IMAGINE   -BY JOHN LENNON

Imagine there's no heaven
It's easy if you try
No hell below us
Above us only sky
Imagine all the people living for today

Imagine there's no countries
It isn't hard to do
Nothing to kill or die for
And no religion too
Imagine all the people living life in peace,

You may say I'm a dreamer
But I'm not the only one
I hope some day you'll join us
And the world will be as one

Imagine no possessions
I wonder if you can
No need for greed or hunger
A brotherhood of man
Imagine all the people sharing all the world,

You may say I'm a dreamer
But I'm not the only one
I hope some day you'll join us
And the world will be as one

28 FRIEND / FRIENDSHIP

There is no pleasure, joy and happiness without friends and friendship. A person whose company is desirable, enjoyable and necessary for you to share your triumphs and glory, joy and happiness, success and achievements is your friend. You forget your loneliness, stresses and tensions, depression and frustration in company of your friend. Friendship can neither be defined nor measured. Friends make your life worthwhile.

Friendship is a relation of equality .A friend never wants to lead you or follow you, he wants to walk besides you in your joy and sorrow, in your glory and adversity. He may not give you advice, solutions or cures but share your pain and touch your wound with warm and tender hands. You can be a friend only if you pack up your status, dignity, prestige, richness, knowledge, university degrees and meet with child like innocence, curiosity, stupidity, truthfulness and without any reservation. Friends, help to multiply your joy by sharing and reduce your woes by sharing.

From childhood we have neighbours, class-mates, school-mates, college-mates, co-travelers in picnics/tours, co-spectators in matches who spend time with us. We meet several people during our service, profession, business with whom we spend time together. We share our past and associated memories. Only few of them become our friends. You can't make real friendship with some intention or motives or purpose. Friendship just happens. Hence we use two different words "Friends" and 'colleagues'. Friend knows your past, believes in your future, and accepts you as you are. Friendship is free advice, free assistance, free patient listener and free company when loneliness kills you and all this as eternal source.

"Birds of same feather flock together" and "Like poles repel unlike poles attract", both the sayings apply to friendship. Some times the friends are so similar in behaviour, thinking, emotions but many times they are diametrically opposite! Friendship is not about finding similarities but respecting the differences as well." You are not my friend because you are like me but because I accept you and respect you as you are."

Arguments and verbal fights often spoil relations even with close relatives. But with friends you can argue and fight without an iota of ill feeling or chance of reducing or loosing friendship. In fact more you argue the closer you are as a friend!

Friendship is an interpersonal relation between two or more people. Bond of friendship is very strong. Mutual understanding, empathy, altruism, mutual trust, joy in each other's company and mainly the relation of real equality are the inherent features of friendship. It gives you freedom to express yourself freely without fear of making mistakes, appearing preposterous, foolish or stupid. To enjoy free laugh, you must have friends. To tell or listen to jokes and enjoy them friends are required. To make fun of each other friend is a must.

Our job, service, profession, business may force us to leave the town/city/state/country in which we are brought up. In the past this resulted in loss of friendship for want of regular contact. Now the time has changed. Telephones, mobile, skype, e-mail, facebook enable us to keep contact with each other wherever you may be. Friendship needs sharing of the time in the past and it's common memories. Now a days people have e-mail and facebook friends without personally meeting each other ever. Only time will tell if such a friendship can develop and last.

In our childhood, teenage, youth, during family life (when we carry responsibilities of a husband/wife, parents, career development), during retired life we develop friendship. Real long lasting friendship develops during your teenage and your bachelour hood days. Friendship with the same gender lasts longer as friendship with opposite gender may lead to sexual attraction and may get converted into marriage.(it is said after marriage the friendship ends!)

We exchange toys in childhood and become friends. Then we play indoor and outdoor games together and develop friendship. Then we share our lunch Tiffin and become friends. We meet in gardens, corridors, parking places, fast food joints, hotels and chat on all the subjects under the sun sowing seeds of friendship. We have party friends—we meet for wet and dry parties. We travel together for picnic, sight- seeing, relaxing and we like our togetherness and then we become friends. We travel together daily for reaching our workplace in a public or private transport—local trains, metros, buses-- chatting together and become friends. We form cricket club, badminton club, playing card groups, senior citizen club, and laughing club, come together under different banners and become friends. One can never tell where and when and how friendship can get formed. Even patients admitted at the same time in a hospital share their grief and become friend. If there is wide difference in language financial status, education, and age then the chances of developing friendship are remote.

Even animals can become friend. There are millions of people having friendship with pets like cats and dogs. People develop friendship with elephants, tigers, lions. One is astonished to see Kevin Richardson rolling on the ground with dozens of his grown-up lion friends. A circus owner presented an elephant to a zoo. After a couple of years he visited the zoo to meet the elephant. People were wonder struck to see the elephant and circus owner hugging each other and tears of joy were running down their cheeks. Animals also have friendship with each other.

Enjoy the pleasant burden of friendship and be happy.

BEST FRIENDS

Once upon a time, there was a royal elephant, which was very well fed and cared for. In the neighbourhood of the elephant shed, there was a scrawny, poorly fed, stray dog. He was attracted by the smell of the rich food being fed to the royal elephant. By eating such rich food, the once underfed dog gradually got bigger and stronger, and became very handsome looking. The good-natured elephant began to notice him. Since the dog had gotten used to being around the elephant, he had lost his fear. So he did not bark at him. Because he was not annoyed by the friendly dog, the elephant gradually got used to him.

Before long, neither would eat without the other, and they enjoyed spending their time together. So it was that they became 'best friends', and wanted never to be separated.

Then one day, a farmer from a remote village, who was visiting the city, passed by the elephant shed. He saw the frisky dog, which had become strong and beautiful. He bought him from the mahout (elephant keeper), even though he didn't really own him. He took him back to his home village, without anyone knowing where that was.

Of course, the royal elephant became very sad, that he didn't want to do anything, not even eat or drink or bathe. So the mahout had to report this to the king, although he said nothing about selling the friendly dog.

It just so happened that the king had an intelligent minister who was known for his understanding of animals. So he told him to go and find out the reason for the elephant's condition.

The wise minister went to the elephant shed. He noticed that there was nothing wrong with elephant's health except he was very sad. Then he enquired with the guards and attendants and learnt that the dog which had become best friend of the elephant, was sold by mahout to an unknown farmer. The minister immediately issued the order through the king that the person who has taken the dog from elephant's shed must return it immediately or he will be punished. The scared farmer immediately returned the dog to elephants shed. Elephant and dog were very happy after reunion. Elephant started eating, drinking, swimming as usual with his friend and recovered within no time.

Learnings:-Friend is the best medicine for loneliness, sadness, depression, sorrow, and apathy.